PRAISE FOR

LET THE
CHILDREN
Pray

The prophecy of Joel that God will pour out His Spirit on all flesh, His sons and daughters young and old, is being more fully realized now. Here in Japan, children are praying. They are the hope for future revival in a most difficult country to evangelize. Hallelujah!

Paul K. Ariga
PRESIDENT, ALL JAPAN REVIVAL MISSION
SUMA-KU KOBE, JAPAN

I heartily endorse *Let the Children Pray*. The exuberance, joy of participation, freshness of content and courage of expression of praying children is infectious. God has blessed Esther Ilnisky with a great love, understanding and belief in children and their power in prayer before Almighty God. May God bless you through this new offering, even as He uses the power of children's prayers for His eternal purposes in these last days!

Luis Bush
INTERNATIONAL DIRECTOR, AD2000 & BEYOND
COLORADO SPRINGS, COLORADO

As I read these pages I saw the marvelous emerging army of the Lord made up of children from every nation. With a fervency and zeal for the Father's house, each of these young warriors is a house of prayer moving forward in the light of Christ. This is an excellent work full of wisdom and insight into the lives and hearts of our children.

Bobbye Byerly
DIRECTOR OF PRAYER AND INTERCESSION, WORLD PRAYER CENTER
COLORADO SPRINGS, COLORADO

Esther Ilnisky is a remarkable woman who carries a profound prophetic message for the Church. Having both witnessed her impact on our own congregation and written of her ministry in *God's Vision for Your Church*, I am delighted that many more can now benefit from her words through this important book. Her refreshing style and uncommon insights hit the mark. *Let the Children Pray* is a gift that will bring help and hope to parents, pastors, teachers and children's workers around the world.

David Cannistraci
PASTOR, EVANGEL CHRISTIAN FELLOWSHIP
SAN JOSE, CALIFORNIA

Esther Ilnisky's *Let the Children Pray* is refreshingly different and utterly fascinating. This book is powerful, pertinent and poignant. I recommend it wholeheartedly.

Joy Dawson
INTERNATIONAL BIBLE TEACHER AND AUTHOR
TUJUNGA, CALIFORNIA

Let the Children Pray will help shake the generations for God.

Cindy Jacobs
COFOUNDER, GENERALS OF INTERCESSION
COLORADO SPRINGS, COLORADO

The principles in this book changed my life. I had been in the Church for many years, but it wasn't until I was taught simple keys to intercession and spiritual warfare that my life was forever marked by God.

Daniel Jacobs
GENERALS OF INTERCESSION
COLORADO SPRINGS, COLORADO

The Word of God says your sons and daughters shall prophesy. The key to fulfillment of this Scripture is teaching our children to pray. *Let the Children Pray* will encourage you to be a part of helping the next generation arise as mighty prayer warriors.

Chuck D. Pierce
PRESIDENT, GLORY OF ZION INTERNATIONAL
COLORADO SPRINGS, COLORADO

Esther Ilnisky's vast experience in teaching children to pray has netted fantastic worldwide results. As she chronicles some of those exciting breakthroughs, we are encouraged and challenged as parents and alerted as church members to listen to the praying children. None seem too young to pray big-time prayers, and what's more, they expect and see results. Esther, thank you for writing this book and for your work with these enthusiastic prayer warriors.

Quin Sherrer
AUTHOR OF *HOW TO PRAY FOR YOUR CHILDREN*
COLORADO SPRINGS, COLORADO

Esther Ilnisky understands the power of children's prayers, and no one has mobilized more children to pray for their world. Her leadership has touched an entire generation of young prayer warriors who have boldly broken through the enemy lines to see God's Kingdom advance on the earth. *Let the Children Pray* is a rare opportunity for the Body of Christ to learn how we all can release our children to change the world.

C. Peter and Doris Wagner
WORLD PRAYER CENTER
COLORADO SPRINGS, COLORADO

LET THE
CHILDREN
Pray

HOW GOD'S YOUNG
INTERCESSORS ARE
CHANGING THE
WORLD

ESTHER ILNISKY

Regal

A Division of Gospel Light
Ventura, California, U.S.A.

Published by Regal Books
A Division of Gospel Light
Ventura, California, U.S.A.
Printed in U.S.A.

Regal Books is a ministry of Gospel Light, an evangelical Christian publisher dedicated to serving the local church. We believe God's vision for Gospel Light is to provide church leaders with biblical, user-friendly materials that will help them evangelize, disciple and minister to children, youth and families.

It is our prayer that this Regal book will help you discover biblical truth for your own life and help you meet the needs of others. May God richly bless you.

For a free catalog of resources from Regal Books/Gospel Light, please contact your Christian supplier or contact us at 1-800-4-GOSPEL or www.regalbooks.com.

Cover Design by Kevin Keller
Interior Design by Rob Williams
Edited by W.G. Simon

Library of Congress Cataloging-in-Publication Data
Ilnisky, Esther, 1929–
   Let the children pray / Esther Ilnisky.
      p. cm .
   Includes bibliographical references.
   ISBN 0-8307-2524-5
   1. Church work with children. 2. Children—Religious life.
   3. Prayer—Christianity. I. Title.

BV639.C4 I46 2000   00-020503
259'.22—dc21

1 2 3 4 5 6 7 8 9 10 11 12 13 14 15 16 17 18 19 20 / 05 04 03 02 01 00

Rights for publishing this book in other languages are contracted by Gospel Literature International (GLINT). GLINT also provides technical help for the adaptation, translation and publishing of Bible study resources and books in scores of languages worldwide. For further information, contact GLINT, P.O. Box 4060, Ontario, CA 91761-1003, U.S.A. You may also send e-mail to Glintint@aol.com, or visit their website at www.glint.org.

Dedicated to the millions of awesome, anointed praying children worldwide, and posthumously to my precious father and mother.

CONTENTS

PART ONE
Through the Eyes of an Adult

Why coach and liberate children to intercede? God is calling them to global vision, to petition Him on behalf of their generation. Children are birthed with eternal prayer potential for such a time as this. With proper coaching in the Lord, children are quick to declare, "Prayers are us! We're not just cute! We're mighty prayer warriors!"

When praying children are given room to interact with teens and adults, not just given rooms in a church building, they become living bridges in reconciling the generations. It's not surprising to hear a child pray, "A ka-jillion [families] is a lot, but [God] can do it!"

How can a parent or spiritual leader learn to mentor and release their children to become the happiest children on earth through grace-gifted prayer? You'll be surprised how simple it is! As one family discovered, "Help! What do we do with our son now? All he wants to do is pray!"

PART THREE
Through the Eyes of God

PRAYER BETWEEN A

Father and Son

HOW A DAD SEES PRAYER

Let the Children Pray is the book that's been missing from my shelf. In my office, I have a multitude of books on prayer: intercessory prayer, pastors praying together, warfare prayer, prayer and fasting; corporate prayer, praying for broken families, and prayers for the nations. All of these books are wonderful, and most have been useful to me at one time or another.

But Esther has developed an area of prayer that we all need more of. In highlighting the prayers of children, this book captures a segment, a resource, a "ready asset" for prayer that is often overlooked in our families and churches. With a genuine excitement that is both refreshing and instructive, Esther reminds us that the prayers of children bring and bind us together as families, that children's prayers have an inspiring innocence and that children can be instruments of God's teaching and revelation.

My oldest son, Marcus, is a testament to Esther's contribution to the Body of Christ. Partly because of her focus on children's prayers, Marcus has had ample opportunity to explore prayer, to exercise his prayer life and to learn what it means to communicate with a holy and gracious God.

As is Esther's way, she has asked Marcus to share with you how he's grown in prayer. What he has to say is a fitting introduction to this book—a book that is sure to expand all of our horizons on children and prayer.

PASTOR TED HAGGARD
New Life Church
Colorado Springs, CO 80921

HOW A SON SEES PRAYER

I grew up listening to my dad pray. At church, in family meetings, at funerals, in practically every event where prayer is involved, my dad is invited to lead. And I love that. I love the memories of Dad coming into my room to pray with me before I went to sleep. Even today when I'm falling asleep in bed, I can listen as Mom and Dad go from room to room tucking my sister and three brothers into bed, sometimes telling them a story— but always saying a prayer. Prayer is in the culture of our family.

Three years ago when I was in Africa, I saw firsthand why my parents wanted all of us to know how to pray. My father and I were traveling around in Tanzania, attending church meetings along the way. We arrived in Dar es Salaam and went to a meeting where my dad was to speak on local church ministry.

After the service a man came up to my dad and told him a story. He told of a man who had died on a small island near where we were staying. The man was very well known, and the whole town attended his funeral. One of the people who attended the funeral was a local pastor. While the pastor was standing in the crowd, God told him to go and pray for the man, and that by doing this the man would be raised from the dead. Unfortunately, the pastor did not have the faith to go, and the burial continued. After the funeral, several of the men from the local church got together and found that the same thing had happened to each of them, but none of them had obeyed.

The story had a sad ending, but it impacted me very much. It showed me that prayer has power, just like in the stories in the Bible, but that people must take action. These men did not act on the power God had given them, so much was lost. This event changed much of the way I perceived the spiritual world from that point on, and the effects would show themselves in years to come.

Recently, I went to Nepal on a missions trip sponsored by our church. The trip was quite adventurous and strewn with constant attacks from the enemy. Our journey took us to a leper colony—a small congregation of people who were excluded from normal society. The lepers were confined to a walled-in area that covered about two acres. These people knew no love and had lost all hope of a better life.

Their meek existence moved our team's hearts, but what could we do? How could we help people who can receive no physical form of comfort? How could we even minister to them emotionally since we didn't speak their language? We were left with two ways, which, as God has it, are the best. First, we had to show them God's love. And second, we had to pray.

And pray we did. Some kids walked around praying, while the others went to individual people, praying healing and life into their broken bodies and dead souls. We prayed in faith; and as we prayed, a deep connection grew between the team and the people. We became friends with them; as more and more became Christians, we became family as well.

As we left the colony, we knew that we had done God's will. God's joy had replaced their sorrow, and God's life had replaced their death. But none of this would have happened without the fervent prayers of the team. It was the heartfelt cries from this group of teenagers that was *sine qua non* to the success of the trip. We saw the sick healed and other miracles happen. And none of it could have taken place without the power that resulted from our prayers.

I'll conclude with the story of a prayer meeting that was held at our church. I walked into it by chance, but soon found that I was there for a purpose. As I began to pray, God started laying deep burdens upon my heart, burdens which I could not ignore. I didn't know what to do with them, so I began to pray. I prayed hard and soon found that that was the purpose of the burdens— they were there to encourage my heartfelt prayer for specific things.

Near the end of the meeting, I was praying for one of my friend's dad, and something happened inside of me. It seemed that God had welled up every passion I had ever felt and dropped them all into my stomach. The words flowed to the point that I was just feeling emotions and letting the word come out. God was moving inside of me and I was overwhelmed. As they handed me the microphone, I broke down in tears. God's power was too much for me to understand, so I just went with it. I started praying for our generation, the relationship between us and our parents and our relationship with God.

God wanted me there that night; He wanted me to represent the people there in prayer. God does not need prayers from people who are considered intelligent or wise, people who can speak fluently or are great public speakers, but from people who feel and pray from their hearts. It does not matter who you are or what you have done: God hears the prayers of those whose hearts are with Him, people who are not ashamed to cry out to God from their hearts.

What astonished me the most was God was using me—a teenage boy who is just learning the many lessons of life, who likes to ride a snowboard and spend time with his friends but who also loves to pray. Perhaps, that is all it takes—a love for prayer.

When I was 12, I went with my dad and some friends to the Global Consultation on World Evangelization in Seoul, South Korea, to pray with Esther Ilnisky and students from all over the world who were involved in the global prayer movement. My dad was a delegate representing the United States, and I went as an intercessor for the conference. At the conference, we prayed for the adults as they met to strategize for the growth of the Church. Afterwards, we made ourselves available for personal ministry to the participants. Then suddenly, the lights went on inside of me. I finally understood how prayer changes the world, prayer opens the door for God's light, and prayer is that incredible common bond shared between every kid and his father—between me and my dad.

This book will do for you what that conference did for me. The lights will come on.

You will love this book.

MARCUS HAGGARD, 16

ACKNOWLEDGMENTS

I want to thank my husband, Bill, for being my
guardian, closest friend, greatest encourager and fan
and my pastor for 45 years. I want to thank him as well
for his faith in me and his desire that I pursue my personal calling, along with the call we have answered and
shared together.

I want to thank my daughter, Sarah, who lavishes me
with TLC and builds me up at just the right moments,
for sharing this project with me. We've laughed, cried
and worked to make it the best we can together.

I appreciate my big brother and four sisters and their
families for believing in me, keeping me in their daily
prayers and appreciating my calling.

I am thankful for my faithful friend and confidant, Mary Tome, for being there endlessly, and for her impeccable PR. Her wise counsel has been key in bringing the adventure to where it is.

My heart is grateful to David Schnorr, CGPM International Director, and his family; the McClures; Karen Moran, our former director and her family; Sherri Rubin; Michelle, who was my first volunteer and who is still giving; and my other faithful staffers, volunteers and teams worldwide who keep me going and are themselves running hard with the vision.

I am indebted to the body of Lighthouse Christian Center International—elders, deacons and congregation—for their support in releasing me to do this work and for diligently covering me with their prayers, words from the Lord and encouragement.

I also want to thank those who comprised my Task Force, the Wednesday Prayer Group and my faithful intercessors, like Nedra, who listen, give guidance and encouragement, and pray daily for the ENI and me.

I can't forget to say thanks as well to Jesse, who started me on this unexpected joyride, along with Lindsay, Katelin and Lacey.

Most of all, I am thankful to the God of all grace, for the adventure, for going before me to dispel my fears, for His forgiving my times of reluctance. In utter dependence on Him, I've cried, *God, You know this is Your idea, so I'll show up if You will . . . please?* He's there every time (toting a bag full of surprises to boot!), and His presence and workings ceaselessly humble, reassure and astound me.

VERY BIG "SMALL"
Beginnings

Where there is no vision, the people perish.

PROVERBS 29:18, *KJV*

God is going to launch you [Esther].

MY HUSBAND, BILL

A SURPRISE VISIT FROM GOD

Who, where, when, why, what and how God decides—*God decides.* No question. Surprise is much too bland a word to describe what happened in the middle of a rather nondescript day in 1983. Not feeling too great, I had sequestered myself in my office. Having to think about too many mundane matters—what to fix for dinner, don't forget to wash clothes, buy dog food, etc., had given me a dull headache. I laid my head on the desk. I was miles away from spiritual mode.

No matter. Suddenly God's presence filled the room. I couldn't move. He said nothing, but He showed me things to come. The vision came in three frames. In the first, I saw many children in our church sanctuary moving swiftly among the congregation, praying with great power for the people. They seemed unaware of earthly concerns. Their voices were authoritative, their eyes reflected the fire of God, their very beings were full of His presence. Praying, praying!

Then a child would stand before the congregation and expound the Word with wisdom far beyond his years. Another would come forth with mighty intercession. One after another, they would pray, expound, prophesy, teach and war against Satan, the power of God rushing through them. Miracles, signs and wonders followed as people fell weeping to their knees to confess their sin, to be healed, to be set free.

After a time, as children do, they became playful—singing, praising and dancing about in celebration—still oblivious to their physical surroundings. Exuberant joy like I'd never heard expressed spread throughout the congregation and *many* joined the celebration.

In the third frame, He showed me what the vision symbolized. The church was the world. The people, a massive host from every tongue, tribe and nation! The children were a praying army full of God's power, setting captives free in Jesus' mighty name! The celebration, a party in heaven, was a tumult—people from every tongue, tribe and nation who had been touched in some way by the children had found entrance there.

This vision from God was potent. I cherished what God had revealed, but the Lord wasn't quite finished in His preparations with my heart. There was still more to come. The Lord would use my mother's legacy of prayer to move me forward as well.

MOTHER'S "SIT DOWN, HONEY"

Mother lived in our home for 10 of the last 11 of her 92 years. For me, now a pastor's wife, leisurely times at home were rare. Having asked her not to close her door when she prayed, I would steal many brief moments to stand at the entrance of this "battle station" to listen, watch, absorb as she called out to God. Over and over, in perpetual motion, I'd stretch out my arms, grasp her prayers from the air and pull them close to my heart. Little did I know the full reason.

One day she ordered, "Sit down, honey." I always knew something weighty was up at times like this. "My bedroom," she began intently, "has been a prayer room since you were a child. Now, you will go to the nations to teach others, from the youngest to the oldest, to intercede for the world. You were named 'Esther' for such a time as this." Then, with the laying on of hands, she passed on her prayer mantle to me. It was our final session.

Shortly thereafter, Esther Network International (ENI) for global intercession was birthed. Our Worldwide Simultaneous 12-Hour Prayer Gatherings became visible in the growing Worldwide Prayer Movement. I began traveling extensively, just as Mother had prophesied, to conduct Corporate Prayer Gatherings and Do-and-Teach Prayer Workshops for both leadership and laity.

This was the beginning, but God was to bring even more goodness into my life. The next voice to exhort me came from my own husband.

A LAUNCH OR A LOUNGE?

"It's very big!" I know the words will be my epitaph; I've said them often enough.

Small and big, are, of course, relative terms. In my naïveté, I assessed ENI to be really big. However, The Worldwide Prayer Movement was gaining such monumental momentum that, by comparison, my "big" was definitely peanuts.

On one particular occasion, I had just returned home after quite a long and intense itinerary. I remember exclaiming to my husband, "The prayer revival for this end time is very big!"

However, my husband was thinking in terms larger than ENI. He replied, "Esther, get some intercessors. God is going to launch you."

This was the last thing I wanted to hear. We had served nearly 20 years as missionaries to Jamaica and Lebanon. Having had 40 years of productive, fruitful ministry by this time, the "big," for me, was as big as I cared to have it. As much as I love and respect this astute man of God, I was really miffed.

"Launch me?" I asked, rather sarcastically. "No, thank you. I don't want to be launched. I'm happy just to be here with you and the church. I'm dreaming of chaise-lounging in the Florida sun. And you're telling me I'm going to be launched?"

"Yes, Esther, launched."

God pursued this further with me a few days later. In another unwelcome encounter a lady, a perfect stranger, whose name tag read "Nedra" had approached me during a meeting break in a ladies room with this unsolicited message: "Esther, this is a strange place for this, but I followed you in here to tell you God says I'm to be one of your intercessors."

Nedra became the first of many intercessors to follow. Some time later, she gifted me with a needlepoint plaque. The words are a constant reminder that God's plans are bigger than my own and I should be willing to follow.

I compliantly hung the plaque in a conspicuous spot. It simply reads, "YES, LORD."

MY LAUNCH OVER LUNCH

One day, Dr. Wagner, who at the time was the International Director of the AD2000 and Beyond Movement United Prayer Track had asked for a meeting to discuss the possibility of ENI joining the track.

Of course, I was willing to do so. Eventually, we were able to cram in a meeting during Dr. Wagner's intense speaking schedule. I knew we had to talk because it was a serious decision to make.

The introductory conversation with Dr. Wagner, his wife, Doris, their daughter Becky and several others had been warm and wonderful, just like the Wagners always are. I felt at ease—even an unexpected affinity to them. I could smell that something was up.

I had said earlier to Mary, who accompanied me, "You know, I'm such a new kid on the block. Dr. Wagner already has a roster of heavyweights with him. I really haven't a clue what we have to offer."

It didn't take long to find out. To me, it was a pretty short trip for such a long-term deal! Dr. Wagner asked about my childhood, about my background, my husband, family, our ministry and ENI. I told him, almost incidentally, that I had learned to pray as a small child. The fact that children were always included in our prayer gatherings obviously intrigued him. Then I asked the big question: "Dr. Wagner, what about the children?"

Whiz bang! Just like that, something instantly clicked in the man. In Mrs. Wagner, too. And in everyone else there. Except, maybe, me. But the matter was settled.

The AD2000 and Beyond Movement United Prayer Track would have a children's subtrack. After a 30-second happy hour over the deal, they all disappeared, going on to the next thing, leaving Mary and me in the dust, so to speak.

"Launch? Oh, *now* I get it!" In retrospect I call it my "before and after Dr. Wagner" phenomenon, but more importantly God's plans proved bigger than I could ever imagine.

Yes, indeed. After weeks on my face before the Lord, and with "pushers" on my trail, I finally embraced the matter that ENI would become part of something larger that God was doing in the world.

In my office are my trinity of signs, the signs of the times that hug and hound me constantly. The first reads, "You don't have time to be astonished." Another reminder, this one under the glass on my desk, badgers me with "Quantum leaps are not for wimps." Oh, but the best challenge is from Nedra's gift. The ever-present "YES, LORD" needlepoint makes everything perfectly clear.

From these events and reminders our Children's Global Prayer Movement was birthed. The CGPM exploded while my comfort zone imploded.

Oh, well, good-bye chaise lounge . . . for such a time as this!

PART ONE

THROUGH THE
EYES OF AN
Adult

CHAPTER 1

INDISPENSABLE
Coaching

[Jesus] called a little child and had him stand among them. And he said:
"I tell you the truth, unless you change and become like little children, you will
never enter the kingdom of heaven. Therefore, whoever humbles himself like this child
is the greatest in the kingdom of heaven. And whoever welcomes a little child
like this in my name welcomes me."

MATTHEW 18:2-5

We thought we would be the generation to possibly usher in the Lord's return.
But He's looking for adults who will die to self, train up the children, and let them lead.

EPISCOPAL PRIEST

COACHED AND LIBERATED

As parents and teachers we have a critical role in *mentoring* our children. We also have the privilege to *release* our children by allowing

PRAYING

CHILDREN

HAD HIGH

VISIBILITY

IN GREAT

AWAKENINGS

AND UNUSUAL

MOVES OF

GOD IN

THE PAST.

them to become prayer warriors for God. Merriam-Webster's Collegiate Dictionary, 10th edition, defines "mentor" as a "coach" and "release" as "to set free from restraint." Do we coach our children, nurture them, cultivate them to pray daily? Do we set our children free from restraints, liberate them and allow them to pray with us?

I highly esteem this generation of children. They are very important to me. They are *altogether* important to God. They are important, *period*. I have great regard for dads and moms who determine to raise godly children. Teaching them to pray from the time they can talk, I believe, is key to everything ahead in their lives and in the world.

What I am sharing I've learned from my teacher, the Holy Spirit, and from interacting with praying children. Coaches are indispensable in freeing children to pray, but in a sense *children* have taught *me* how to coach them by their love, honesty and simplicity. When children are free to pray, they become history makers.

It's a given. Praying children had high visibility in great awakenings and unusual moves of God in the past. With the spirit of supplication upon them, their prevailing prayer reportedly hastened revival. I document a few examples in this book; but more importantly, praying children are making history today, shaping the present and future for end-time revival and harvest.

The Freedom to Pray

Why coach and liberate children to intercede? To cooperate with God, first of all. He has put a desire in them to pray. Think about this: If youth and children are now making up half the world's population, then I believe half the Christian world's prayer warriors should be youth and children, say, one quarter each. It makes me feel *responsible* to coach and liberate them. How about you?

We discovered early on that the Holy Spirit is carrying out God's plans for this generation of children. Couple that with a healthy reverential fear of the Lord that I and my teams carry with us whenever we're with your children! It's a sacred trust that is not taken lightly.

With this predestined anointing on them to pray, natural or supposed time and age limitations are literally defied. *If given the opportunity, children will pray for hours and are so enveloped in the blessing that even games, drinks or snacks are long forgotten. Even bathroom breaks are short. Not that they pray long prayers; they just pray* more *prayers.*

For example, take those children's workers who are admittedly shocked that children with a supposed 10-minute attention span would pray, literally, for hours. I've been shocked, too, when it comes to children and prayer; some data doesn't seem to compute. I get my natural mind out of the way; I just patiently watch, agree, wait, listen to the Holy Spirit and, with sensitivity,

allow the children to call the shots. I follow their signals. I really
have no theoretical explanation for what happens. It just does.

I love this terrific problem one dad and mom faced with
their son, Billy. "Whenever we ask him to pray over a meal, he
goes on and on and on about everything. The food is slowly dete-
riorating; so is everyone's patience. What do we do?" Sound
familiar? If a child desires to pray, that child will pray whenever
the opportunity arises.

When Billy is asked to lead in prayer *only at mealtime*, his I-
get-to-pray mind-set, his I-get-to-pray button, gets pushed. It's
the only time he sees his prayers as valid, so he goes for it! You
have a choice: unleash that prayer power at more appropriate
times—and plenty of them—in order to satisfy his desire to pray,
or just get used to cold mashed potatoes.

*I believe godly children are the most untapped resource of prayer
today, both in the home and in the Church worldwide.* Nurturing the
prayer potential of children could free them, free parents and
free the Church from the very fears for them that cause us all
such grave concern. Equipping and liberating them to use godly
authority over evil powers could transform them, you, your
home and the Church and could ultimately revolutionize the
world.

One mother wrote this wonderful example of godly coaching and releasing:

> I was praying in my bedroom when my three-year-old
> daughter, Lauren, came in and lay on the floor next to
> me. I asked her to leave because this was my time with
> the Lord. The Holy Spirit immediately checked me, that
> I should teach her everything I had learned, and to
> include her, because her spirit is the same as mine. So, I
> told her she could pray with me. She prayed the most

profound prayer I've ever heard. She's now eight and is still at it!

That's coached and liberated!

I hope this, in essence, is your story, too. Can you capture the big picture? Multiply this story by the thousands of dads and moms, grandparents, pastors and children's workers who've had a "check from the Spirit" with their children. Imagine the results of freeing their children to pray and how it impacted and changed their homes, churches and lives.

Blockbusters and Spiritual Abortions

"Esther, you must write your book about praying children. It'll be a blockbuster!" The remark came from a highly regarded friend, but the words were a playback from a previous nudge by the Lord, by my husband and from close friends to write such a book.

The world "blockbuster" really struck me. I'm all for taking the word in its cliché form. Absolutely. For the sake of praying children. Superimposed over that, however, would have to be my highest aspiration—that it will "bust some blocks." Religious blocks. Intellectual blocks. Blocks of accepted man-made traditions and teachings. Blocks of opinions and judgments about what praying children of all cultures can or cannot, should or should not, do.

These blocks lead to spiritual abortion, too. Knowing the intrinsic value of human life, God's highest creation, we're diligent to look after our children's temporal physical and emotional needs. To feed and clothe them. To educate them well. Children are lavished with nourishment of the very best quality, but they, too, are SPIRIT, soul and body. *If children's spirituality is either never discerned or not allowed to function, it is to me, then, aborted. Consequently, the family, the Church and the world are robbed of a multitude of precious, valuable spiritual gifts; uppermost in my mind is the power of the children's prayers—to say nothing of aborted potential answers because of those aborted prayers.*

These thoughts were sparked one day while in the anteroom of a pastor's office where my team and I had gone to pray, to prepare for our ministry in the church. I had been feeling bewildered and defeated having just left an assignment where I thought we'd gotten absolutely nowhere. The children, who I saw as would-be mighty prayer warriors, have been hidden away, engrossed in games and toys to help grow their lives. Valuable tools, most certainly. Yet it seemed there was nothing we could do to *bust the block of tradition,* which basically left out of the picture the children's capacity to make a contribution, to utilize this God-given power to be full-fledged prayer warriors for their generation, to respond to the spirit of supplication upon them.

I didn't want it to happen again. Suddenly, I heard myself blurt out, "It's spiritual abortion!" I thought, *I believe the Holy Spirit is speaking to me. I don't want that to happen here.* (In my walk with God, I've come to recognize those times when unpremeditated words come forth. They've always been to teach and grow me. I walk softly with this thought.)

The events that day still make me ask three questions:

- Are children's powerful prayers being aborted today?
- Do our godly children have the right and the freedom to confront the spirits of this present darkness that are out to destroy them?
- In trying to shelter our children from the world, might we in reality be leaving them vulnerable to it?

Wary adults sometimes remark, "You know, Esther, they're a little young for *that.*" By "that," they mean deeper levels of prayer where they're exposed to the Holy Spirit in an even fuller measure that makes adults feel somewhat uncomfortable. (Perhaps, those adults haven't been there themselves.) To which I repeatedly respond, "Tell me, *how early on in life are they exposed to the unholy spirit?*"

I want to make it perfectly clear that I do not minimize the role of a parent or teacher in the life of a child. In fact, I continually maximize it. I do want to point out, however, that even the prophet Samuel at a very young age was aware of God's presence (see 1 Sam. 3), but the boy knew to go to Eli, the high priest, for instruction and clarification. The adult role is to instruct, clarify and protect the child, but also to allow and encourage the child to freely communicate with God as Eli did with Samuel.

GREAT COACHES IN THE CHURCH

As adults we can never underestimate the role we have in coaching children to be liberated in praying to the Lord. One of the cornerstones of godly coaching came through my experiences with my family at church. My rich childhood memories of being allowed to pray, to intercede with adults, remains a wonderful heritage in my life.

As a child, I vividly recall the sound of fervent supplications from the faithful saints at The Gary Full Gospel Tabernacle. They prayed for the lost and their prayers rose as incense to heaven. Everyone—and I do mean everyone—gathered systematically, day after day, week after week, year after year, for unhurried seasons of prayer, weeping for the lost. *Souls. Lost souls.* All the sights and sounds are alive still.

We heard about those souls, too, from missionaries serving in faraway lands whose fervid prayer appeals moved me deeply. Pictures of the lost jumped out at me from their slides. Often the last slide shown, predictably a setting sun, stamped an indelible urgency on my young heart to pray, pray, pray before it's too late. *It has been harvestime ever since I can remember.*

My church was a superb school of prayer for me. My many loving teachers imparted endless truths to me that stuck hard. Even the lyrics to a song, "Jesus loves the little children, all the children of the world. Red and yellow, black and white" taught me to disavow prejudice and to have a caring, praying heart.

My mother would also declare incessantly, "No weeping saints, no weeping sinners!" I quickly learned to weep for souls along with a mighty host of intercessors. Lost and dying souls. I'd gaze compassionately at pictures of starving, dying children and cry for them. It was good to feel Jesus' heart for them. I learned very early on what standing in the gap was all about. "Intercession" was a familiar word. But the most precious gift of all was that my coaches in prayer helped me, liberated me and caused me to know that *God saw my tears and He heard my childish prayers. That truth gave me indescribable ecstasy.*

CHAPTER 2

THINK OUTSIDE
the Box

The boy ministered before the LORD under Eli the priest.

1 SAMUEL 2:11

THE BALM FOR FAMILY HEALING

"I've never seen my dad and mom—or my pastor—so happy!" Happy indeed! So was the little boy who said it. So were all the pastors, the elders and deacons, the moms and dads, brothers and sisters, aunts and uncles, cousins and friends, grandmas and grandpas. Even the babies were happy! Just because they were *all together*—a blended family of God—in the big church, in an inter-generational prayer gathering. At the precise point of his exclamation, we were celebrating a spectacular victory.

Use your imagination to recapture the moment. An uproarious outburst of praise, victory dancing, streamers waving. Maximum energy, decent and in order, well suited to the occasion. A spacious platform crowded with an assortment of all the above.

Midway through, something so ingenious and spontaneous occurred that everyone knew only the Holy Spirit could have orchestrated it. A group of teenagers on the platform had gone to kneel before the children—some, their younger siblings—weeping and repenting. Asking their forgiveness for not being good examples, for looking down on them, avoiding and ignoring them, for treating them as "nonhuman beings."

Families—entire households—reconciled openly with tears and hugs. Fathers to sons and daughters. Mothers, too. Brothers to sisters. Children to grandparents. Even husbands to wives. Every combination. The entire congregation wept for joy. Grandpas holding bouncing babies skipped around gingerly. Toddlers pranced about happily (they *do* know things).

All the while, I was steeped in my first object lesson in reconciliation between generations. In living color I learned that *a spirit of reconciliation is a natural fruit of intergenerational prayer.* Therefore, intergenerational prayer reconciles the family.

MAKING ROOM FOR THE CHILDREN

Rooms. They separate people. It's necessary, of course, to have enough rooms to accommodate a family. Parents will send children to their rooms for disciplinary reasons. But rooms are, well, so private. Privacy. It's necessary, too, but it can also isolate. Everyone goes off to his own room, unblended.

It's a foregone conclusion that in a church of any size, rooms for children are absolutely essential. Of course. But rooms (structures) tend to unblend and room (offering freedom for children to pray) tends to blend. Although the thought I had one day about making room and not just rooms for the children hit me unexpectedly, it didn't take a second thought for me to fly with it. It simply makes sense.

My husband has an especially unique rapport with the children. He has made room for them in every aspect of the spiritual life of the church. I love to see them hug him and ask, "How's my pastor today?" We care that church to them is less perceived as the *grown-up's* church or the *big* church but, more desirably, as *my* church.

EVER ASK A CHILD WHAT HE OR SHE THINKS ABOUT CHURCH? I HAVE. OFTEN THE ANSWER HAS BEEN "IT'S FOR GROWN-UPS ONLY."

Incidentally, the children have actually *helped* him. For instance, in a church service, he'll ask them to toss GLOBALLS (large, soft globes showing the world, each with "Catch the Vision" written on it) to some disinterested grown-ups and shout "Catch the vision!" Then he sits back and watches what happens. Before you know it, adults who could never before have been persuaded are very prone to "catch it" as they pray and hug the world.

The experts say that whatever attitudes and associations our children develop early on regarding church, church leaders and, ultimately, God, will stay with them for a lifetime. For this reason, it's important to ask ourselves, *What impressions are we leaving with our children when it comes to prayer?*

Ever ask a child what he or she thinks about church? I have. Often the answer has been "It's for grown-ups *only*" or "The preacher preaches and I have to sit still for a long time."

I've been a guest in many very large churches. In interacting with the children, I've discovered some unexpected things. One of the obvious difficulties in churches today is that children don't feel associated with the larger congregation of adults. A typical conversation with children goes something like this (I've used fictitious names):

"Hi, Bobby. Hi, Christy. Hi Rachel. It's great to be here. Pastor Smith invited us."

"Pastor *who?*" Bobby asks quizzically.

"Your church's pastor . . . Pastor Smith."

Bobby replies, "Oh, I didn't know *that* was his name."

Mary interjects, "He's never talked to me" [note the reverse perception].

Rachel chimes in and points to the children's pastor, "Pastor Mike's my pastor."

I respect and honor children's pastors. I've seen and heard their heart for children. Surprisingly, however, I've also heard them express a desire for more togetherness with the "big church" because they feel they and the children are often tolerated as a separate entity.

I recommend to the Church intergenerational prayer, to make the Church a blended family of God. *It's a spiritual function where everyone can interact easily.* In churches of all sizes, it creates an amicable environment to bring all the streams of a church's spiritual life together. Large churches make it work in multiple small-group settings. *Intergenerational prayer is a common denominator to make the Church the blended family of God. The very nature of it reconciles the generations. After all, prayer is prayer, no matter who does the praying or how it's done, as long as it comes from a heart right with God.*

At our intergenerational gathering, Jason, seven, was using our prayer spinner (a game where children spin a dial that falls on different issues related to prayer). When the pointer landed on "Unity," he was asked what it meant.

Jason responded, "People doing things together."

"What kind of people?" he was asked.

"Grown-ups and children doing things together," he said.

The leader of the gathering exclaimed, "Wow! Out of the lips of children."

Blended Families

When parents and adults begin to think outside the box and allow their children to pray with them at home and church, the result is wondrous. Family prayer has a trickle-down effect on every facet of family life, molding a peaceable—even functional—intergenerational household. Here are a few testimonies:

We think twice now before saying, "Okay, Joshua! You, too, David! Go to your rooms and cool off. This minute!" (Their sister, Annie, always dashes to her room on her own whenever this happens.) Now we're working on cooling off together, on our knees.

My church has a "war room" for intercession. I thought to myself, *Gee, with five kids, my whole house is a war zone—*

but not that kind! Well, my husband and I decided to make our family room a war room (like my church's) one night a week. *You know, Esther, letting the children do battle in the heavenlies has given us a little peace on earth!*

I really haven't been a great dad. I guess I'll do more with my family now. I'm going to start by having us pray together, as you suggested.

It's a second marriage for both my husband and me. It's his, my and our kids, but we've never been a real family. Your teaching (on intergenerational prayer) has changed that. We're now hoping to be good examples of the saying, "The family that prays together stays together."

Children also tell their parents, pastors and teachers that they feel better about their siblings when intergenerational prayer is fostered.

Guess what. My big brother is my best friend now. Thank you.

Our children actually have fun together since you did the reconciliation with us.

I just couldn't stand my little sisters before. Now, at least I can tolerate them.

Don't Miss a Child's Moment

Children chat and tug incessantly. Have patience, parents—don't miss a moment of eternal purpose by automatically saying "Stop it!" Discern if the Holy Spirit is at work. You could be missing a miracle waiting to happen. *Children often don't know why they feel an urgency to pray. They just do; so give them room, just let them.* Allowing them to pray, to express themselves toward God, could abort a tragedy that we can't see coming our way.

A godly mother, her seven-week-old baby and Jesus' presence together illustrate intergenerational prayer perfectly. In a workshop in Argentina, a lady with cancer asked for prayer. Everyone gathered around.

At my impromptu instructions, a mother took her baby's hand in hers and placed them both on the woman with cancer. "Oh," the lady exclaimed, "heat from the baby's hand is going through my body!"

The mother simply said, "Thank You, Jesus."

I reiterated as calmly as I could, "This baby, righteous seed, is spirit, soul and body, too."

Shortly afterwards, we received good news that the woman with cancer was healed. That's intergenerational prayer at work!

A Mother + Her Righteous Seed + Jesus = A Miracle

Blended Churches

Whenever even the remotest opportunity arises, I have this conversation with pastors. Wearing a smile and a good mix of cordiality and prayed-for cha m, I ask, "Do you have corporate prayer in your church?"

Their response is usually a casual, "Yes, of course, Esther."

Then I ask, still smiling, "Do you include the children?" After an awkward moment's silence and some foot shuffling, I manage to drag out of them a reluctant, "Well . . . ahem . . . no." Seeing my gotcha grin, they concede to the setup.

To savor my anticipated victory, I jump in with the clincher they're already expecting. I do it for the sake of the children. My modus operandi is definitely not that of a crusader, but "pioneer" has a familiar ring. I continually surprise myself when I ask, "Then your corporate prayer isn't really corporate after all, is it?" My point is usually well received—with a smile in return, thank God! A perfect *selah* (Hebrew word meaning to pause) moment. After which, come to think of it, I seem to get lots of acquiescent pats on the back, the interpretation of which I leave between them and the Holy Spirit.

The intergenerational concept is up and running in the spiritual life of my church. It has been my training base. We're not a megachurch, which logistically can make a difference. However, we're integrated racially, ethnically, socially *and generationally*. It really works!

Blended Gatherings in the Church of the Past

There are a host of examples from history that show how children have been a special part of God's renewal and revival. Remember those who came before us, who made room for the children.

Joshua Did—for a Church Service

He "read to the whole assembly . . . including the women *and children*" (Josh. 8:35, emphasis added).

Jehoshaphat Did—for a Prayer Meeting

He called "the men . . . their wives and children and little ones" to come together for a National Day of Prayer! (2 Chron. 20:13).

Nehemiah Did—for a Celebration
They came "rejoicing. . . . The women *and children* also rejoiced" (Neh. 12:43, emphasis added).

John Wesley Did
He speaks of children being "much affected" and "crying out." He recorded on Monday, September 6, 1773: "Presently the Spirit fell upon . . . [the children], and . . . the Spirit of grace and supplication, till the great part of them were crying together . . . with a loud, bitter cry. . . . I suppose such a visitation of children has not been known in England these hundred years. . . . The fire kindled and ran from heart to heart till few. . . were unaffected. . . . God begins his work in children. Thus it has been in Cornwall, Manchester, and Epworth. Thus the flame spread to those of riper years."[1]

A Group in 1859 on the East Coast of Scotland Did
It was reported in the local press that "a boy of eight . . . under strong convictions, spoke in the meeting, and his words made such a deep impression that more were convicted and converted than on any other occasion."[2]

Jonathan Edwards Did
He observed in the revivals in New England: "Very many little children have been remarkably enlightened, and their hearts wonderfully affected and enlarged, and their mouths opened, expressing themselves in a manner far beyond their years, and to the just astonishment of those which have heard them."[3]

By the same token, in the revivals in other places during the eighteenth century, children were a part of the great move of God. As the Spirit was poured out in Kilsyth, Scotland, children were "awakened." [4]

In periods of revival children came to a deep realization of what God means to them personally. Quite small children can have a great sense of the Divine.

Robert Murray McCheyne Did

He comments that in a revival of 1839, ministers treated children in the same way as adults, with remarkable success: "The ministers . . . have . . . spoken to children as freely as to grown persons. It was commonly at public meetings . . . that children were impressed, often also in their own . . . meetings, when no minister was present." There were many instances of children "prostrated" during the general revival of 1859, night after night. [5]

Blended Gatherings in the Church Today

To me, the cliché about the family that prays together means more than just an immediate family. Think of it in global terms. Numerous reconciliation movements are dedicated to bringing the global Church together. *Intergenerational prayer is key to making the Church worldwide truly blended. We've been there. We've watched it happen.*

God revives an idea and breathes it on the winds of time. Whoever desires to catch it, at that point and time, can do so. That, capsulated, is precisely what I've done. Intergenerational prayer is nothing new. There's just more of it because God wants it, because there are more people on the earth and because more of them are praying.

Australia

This was only the beginning for our community. We have prayed from 18:00 to 06:00 the following morning. We were blessed with not only the children who attended the prayer meeting but there were a lot of adults, too.

Malaysia
Where Oriental culture differs from that of the West, united prayer is reconciling the generations. Our CGPM reps there tell us "the combined prayer meetings are going extremely well. Church leaders and workers came from as far away as 100 miles to learn from us. Many adults were encouraged and when the children were released to pray for them, they were deeply touched."

WHAT ADULTS ARE TO SEE TODAY

A growing number of Church leaders are being challenged by praying children and are making room for them. Just think! *It quite possibly could be the "room" where end-time revival is just waiting to happen.* After all, intergenerational prayer *is doable!*

One international Christian reconciliation movement recognizes our intergenerational prayer as a viable work of reconciliation. Its leader states:

Intergenerational prayer is leading the way to healing broken relationships with efforts that address the wounds that divide the generations. *Intergenerational prayer is most certainly a primary key to transgenerational reconciliation* (emphasis added).

Never underestimate the power of children's prayers. By making room for children in the home, at church and throughout the world, we tap into their power and allow great things to be done in Jesus' name. Reconciliation between family members, different age groups, different ethnic groups and between nations is possible.

I once asked Chad, 10, to interpret Jesus' admonition to His disciples, "Let the little children come to me" (Luke 18:16).

Chad replied, "Let them *pray*. Isn't that how we come to Him now?"

"Yes, Chad."

So we let the children pray. We let them shout "Hosanna!"

At Jesus' triumphal entry into Jerusalem, religious leaders were indignant when the children shouted "Hosanna!" (see Matt. 21:12-16). Jesus rebuked them, with the reminder that the psalmist prophesied that praise would come from children. The passage from Psalm 8:2 continues by saying that babes and sucklings would "silence the foe and the avenger."

I see a second triumphal entry of Jesus rising on the horizon—perfect timing for today's children. Because of the upheaval of violence against children in these tumultuous days, society's cry to "Save the children," takes on deeper meaning. I believe Jesus is literally shouting to the Church, *Let the children shout their own hosannas—O Lord, save us!—to silence their foe and their avenger.*

Yes, we let the children lead. In homes and churches, they lead us, praying prayers that humble us and actually build our faith. I encourage every parent, pastor, teacher and all leaders of children to ponder Isaiah 11:6: "And a little child shall lead them."

Notes

1. Andy and Jane Fitz-Gibbon, *Something Extraordinary Is Happening* (United Kingdom: Monarch, 1995), pp 118, 119.
2. Ibid., p. 119, 120.
3. Ibid.
4. Ibid., p. 120.
5. Ibid.

CHAPTER 3

PRAYING CHILDREN
101

Pray continually.

1 THESSALONIANS 5:17

COACHES WITH QUESTIONS

Every parent, teacher and pastor wants to be a good coach for the children, but there are always a lot of questions as to how we liberate them to pray. I am frequently asked when being interviewed on radio and television or when I talk with parents, pastors and other spiritual leaders how we should release our children to talk to God daily. Here are some answers to those questions:

Q. How valid are children's prayers?
A. As valid as yours and mine . . . perhaps even more so, because of the children's purity, trust and blatant faith.

They don't just believe for answers; they expect miracles! No doubts, no prideful wordiness or clichés, no questions, no religious hang-ups.

Unlike those around Him who tended to devalue children's spirituality, and on at least one recorded occasion shooed children away from Jesus, the Lord affirmed the abilities of children in the areas of spiritual insight, proper attitude toward God, pure desire for God, and praising and worshiping God:

- "I praise you, Father, Lord of heaven and earth, because you have hidden these things from the wise and learned, and revealed them to little children" (Matt. 11:25; Luke 10:21). In these passages the "little children" are those with simple faith who believe in Jesus and His mighty works, including Jesus' victory over Satan.
- "I tell you the truth, unless you change and become like little children, you will never enter the kingdom of heaven. Therefore, whoever humbles himself like this child is the greatest in the kingdom of heaven" (Matt. 18:3,4). Jesus lifts up childlike humility as a requirement for entering the kingdom of heaven.
- "Let the little children come to me, and do not hinder them, for the kingdom of heaven belongs to such as these" (Matt. 19:16; Mark 10:14; Luke 18:16). Jesus commends the desire of children to simply *be* with Him and *be blessed* by Him.
- "Have you never read, 'From the lips of children and infants you have ordained praise'?" (Matt. 21:16, quoting Ps. 8:2). Jesus approves of children's praise and worship being directed toward Himself.

Q. How much of a prayer warrior do the parents/mentors have to be themselves in order to teach and nurture prayer in their children?

A. You don't need to be a serious prayer warrior to encourage and release your children in prayer, but I can guarantee you, encouraging and releasing your children in prayer will be a great impetus to your own prayer life! Experiencing the prayers of children who believe God with simple faith and who trust Him to do mighty things has the power to spark faith in us.

But wherever you are in your Christian walk with God, even if you do not picture yourself as a mighty prayer warrior, the Bible actively teaches you to mentor your children, to be a living demonstration of learning to love and follow God, despite all your imperfections, false starts and (let's be honest) sins. "Love the LORD your God with all your heart and with all your soul and with all your strength. Impress [these commandments] on your children. Talk about them when you sit at home and when you walk along the road, when you lie down and when you get up" (Deut. 6:5,7). As we depend on God's grace for our growth in Christ, God will make it easier to flow with the children and even lead them into deeper prayer experiences.

Q. At what age is it appropriate for children to be introduced to the concept of prayer and global intercession?

A. The sooner the better! From a very early age, our children are bombarded with news of frightening real-life atrocities from around the world and with the belief that no one set of moral values is better than any other.

Why not encourage children to use the tools God has given Christians to deal with a culture that is far from God? I believe children must learn early on to "take it to the Lord in prayer."

Exposure and imitation help. Even Paul the apostle exposed the Corinthians and Philippians with his own example of faith and love and urged them to imitate him (see 1 Cor. 4:16; 11:1; Phil. 3:17), so we need to expose our children to prayer so that they can learn to imitate our example. Children learn to deal with fears, insecurities, and concerns in their families and in other cultures by learning to pray.

When adults talk to God about the world, it makes them feel better. Well, the sooner children get to, the sooner they'll feel better, too. So let them!

Q. Are all children called to be prayer warriors?
A. Are all Christians? I say yes. For example, in the context of putting on the armor of God and fighting against the devil's schemes, Ephesians 6:18 says, "Pray in the Spirit on all occasions with all kinds of prayers and requests." This passage addresses the entire Christian community, not simply adults alone. Although the focus of the New Testament stories is usually on adults, children are not at all left out. The full blessing of God is promised to children (see Acts 2:39) and the presence of children, family members and servants (see Acts 11:14; 16:15,31; 18:8). The Early Church had young people of unspecified ages in meetings (see Acts 12:13,14; 20:9). In one very clear example, the entire church at Cyprus, including children, prayed for Paul and his missionary prayer band (see Acts 21:5). Based on these examples, we can reasonably assume

that in the Early Church, children of believing parents grew up in families full of praise, intercession and spiritual warfare.

I believe it is vitally important that when we teach children about prayer, we diligently teach them about the armor of God. We want children to know without a shadow of a doubt that they have nothing to fear from the devil because "the one who is in you is greater than the one who is in the world" (1 John 4:4), and He has given us perfect spiritual protection from Satan's attacks. Children, like adults, also need to know that God has given believers spiritual authority over the devil (see Matt. 28:18-20; Luke 10:19) and that when we are in God's will, no attack of the enemy can harm us (see 1 John 5:18). Why? Because God has given us His Holy Spirit and, because Jesus is the victor over sin, hell and the grave, even if we die, God promises us eternal life with His Son (see John 3:16; 2 Cor. 5:1-8).

But why stop there? Imagine. One quarter of our world will be under the age of 12 by the year 2000. If we abort children's rights to become prayer warriors, we rob them and us of answered prayer![1]

Actually, since children are the most affected by our sinful world, isn't it preeminently important that they talk to God themselves? They're innocent, born into a perverse society. Perhaps being prayer warriors from the time they can talk frees them early enough on from the curse of victimization.

Q. How much understanding of the spirit realm (godly/ungodly) can children have?

A. The Holy Spirit doesn't have an age. He isn't 5 or 30 or 55. He is Spirit and works in all who believe. Children understand more than they're given credit for. Some just don't yet have the vocabulary to express themselves. They're really sensitive and savvy. We've worked with the gamut of them.

As adults we need to find the right balance between giving children credit for genuine spiritual insight (or visions) and following the silly modern sentiment that true spiritual and moral wisdom can only be found in the hearts of innocent children. The Bible is much more realistic than that, teaching that all of us are tainted by sin (see Ps. 51:1-5; Jer. 17:9) and that true wisdom is a road which must be traveled over one's whole life (Prov. 1:1-9; 22:6). Only by walking in God's grace and by learning responsibility can we teach grace and responsibility. This is what the entire book of Proverbs is about—the adult responsibility of training a child in the way he or she should go, and the child's responsibility to learn from the godly wisdom of his or her elders.

Yet, too often, parents and churches have adopted man-made philosophies and habits with regard to children (i.e., they should be seen and not heard). Some children are left to eat their meals and watch TV while everyone in the family goes to his or her own room—this obviously leaves little sense of community. In some churches, no babies are allowed in the sanctuary, and children are not welcome in the "big" church unless they're performing in some kind of special event.

If children are not given a credible place in the spiritual life of families and churches today, it is possible they will not be prepared to be strong members and leaders in the families and churches of tomorrow.

Q. How about taking the children into deeper levels of intercession and spiritual warfare? Is it healthy or normal? Should parents be concerned for their welfare?

A. "Deep" is a relative word. Parents and pastors get nervous about this. Frankly, so do I when I think too much about it. However, I've had to concede to the Holy Spirit. *The deeper they go, the happier they get! As they go deeper, and as the Spirit leads, the better they cope in their everyday lives. They know there are certain things only God can do anything about, so they dig deep to get into His place.* There, they're in closest proximity to finding peace and joy away from the stormy environment of the world. I've even dared say, "I believe children intercessors are the happiest children on earth!" Don't ask me to explain it. It amazes me, too.

I'm sure you'll agree that today's children are the most informed generation in history. The profusion of data is staggering. A four-year-old is likely to know more than you did as a teenager. There isn't anything anyone can fully protect them from—*except from their adversary* (see Luke 10:19; 1 John 5:18)! So let them go wherever they must in order to settle issues, some of which we may never have had to deal with. I have found that *releasing children to petition God for their generation provides for their own sense of well-being. Let me reiterate: When I ask how they feel after having "gone deeper," they say, "Peaceful. Happy. Good. Great."*

Q. What can adults learn from children's prayers?

A. Interacting with praying children has taught me myriad things about this question, so it's easy to answer. Maintain a repentant and pure heart; keep prayers simple. Stay humble. Avoid religious clichés. Get to the point. Discuss less, pray more. Pray, believing for and expecting answers. Children have blatant faith; they get answers without much effort or fanfare. "Effectual" and "fervent" (see Jas. 5:16, *KJV*) don't necessarily mean lengthy and loud. I think my own prayers are becoming more viable since I've been hanging out with the children; I'm learning to pray like they do. I tell them, "My goal is to be just like you! Jesus said I need to be like a child so that I can enter His kingdom."

Of course, this does not mean that adults should revert to childishness. There's a big difference between childishness and childlikeness. Adults are not to remain spiritual babies but are to "grow up" into our salvation (see Eph. 4:15; 1 Pet. 2:2); we are to "put childish ways behind [us]" and become responsible, loving adults (see 1 Cor. 13:11); we are to "stop thinking like children" (1 Cor. 14:20) and be transformed in our thinking by Christ (see Rom. 12:1,2). In addition, adults have the responsibility to provide for and protect the children under their care (see 2 Cor. 12:14; 1 Thess. 2:7,11), even to the point of disciplining them (see Heb. 12:5-8).

What adults do gain from children is simplicity, directness and an uncomplicated belief in God's ability to answer supplications.

Q. Do you teach children about fasting and prayer?
A. Absolutely. Why not? With parental supervision, they can fast a meal now and then? We also encourage them to occasionally abstain from dessert or TV or video games, or whatever else they decide to fast.

During the media blitz showing Ethiopia's masses of starving children, Ashley, six, would cry and refuse to eat when she saw pictures of them. Her parents asked me to talk with her. "Ashley," I said, "you have a caring heart, just like Jesus. You can use it to help. Your family can pray together instead of eating a meal. You can cry for those children. It's called fasting and praying. Then, I think you'll be able to eat all your meals; but Jesus wants you to keep on praying."

I asked her family to experience her spirituality with her. It worked! All the family fasted and prayed with her. (It was a first for them all.) Outcome? "We've never seen Ashley so happy. We're happier, too. It was so great, we're going to do it again."

Q. What do you think about children praying for adults?

A. Praying children eagerly desire to lay hands on and pray for anyone within reach.

In the New Testament, Jesus laid his hands on children and blessed them (see Matt. 19:15; Mark 10:16). Jesus healed the blind and other sick people (see Mark 8:23-25; Luke 4:40). People received the Holy Spirit through laying on of hands (see Acts 8:17; 9:12,17), and the apostles healed through touch (see Acts 28:8). Certainly in these informal acts of touching, the children may be included.[2]

God obviously put the desire to pray for others in them—another one of His brilliant ideas. Incidentally, while they do it, a heap of opinions and judgments get trampled on. Better still, pastors and churches are transformed right before everyone's disbelieving eyes! *Recognizing that children's prayer power is divinely inherent sets everyone free to accept and utilize it.*

I watched intently as the praying children of GCOWE '95 hovered over Dr. Wagner. He had come to our war room to ask the children to pray for him. All 40 children converged on him, wanting to touch him. They prayed; they prophesied; they exhorted and even warned him against sin. This distinguished man of God, a leader among leaders, *let them.*

No one had the faintest idea what God had up His sovereign sleeve this time, when about a dozen children, hand-picked by the Lord, had come with their parents to a conference. I was conducting workshops at a Harvest Evangelism conference where three fiery evangelists from Argentina were preaching. Ed Silvoso asked me to gather any children I could find for the laying on of hands right alongside the evangelists! While these anointed men of God ministered, the anointed children did too, laying hands on and sometimes prophesying to about 100 adults who had stood patiently in line, some for over an hour to receive ministry from them. A sign and wonder. For many, it was a first.

I regularly ask children to pray for me. I am probably the number one blessed person alive simply because children love to pray blessings. Here is what I often hear:

- "Dear Lord, just bless and bless Miss Esther with lots of good surprises."
- "God, You are going to take Miss Esther to lots of places to teach adults about us, aren't You?"
- "Oh, dear Jesus, keep Miss Esther safe on all the trips she takes. She's very important to us and she's going to be more important to our dads and moms and pastors, too." (I can live with that.)

Our church children literally swarm around my pastor/husband to pray for him, too; they give him the word of the Lord. Little hands fight to touch him on his head, his belt buckle, knees, feet, to bless—and sometimes exhort—him. Early one Sunday morning his three-year-old prayer partner jumped on his lap to "tell him something from God." Though she had absolutely no clue what the word meant, with her grandmother's help syllable by syllable, she blurted, "Pastor, God says, 'Stop pro-cras-ti-na-ting.'" Well, it hit the spot and he delivered a long overdue message to his congregation that resulted in a mighty move of God that day. Y-YES!

Q. What about when you think you've blundered?
A. Blundered? Blunders do inevitably and unpredictably happen. Thankfully, the Holy Spirit doesn't blunder. When *we* do, He comes to the rescue, graciously blanketing our flaws and foibles.

An assignment, for example, can appear to have all the components of a disaster—lack of preparedness, order, discipline, help; distractions—and many times, things beyond anyone's control. I always take full responsibility for the events in these situations. It releases our hosts. Afterwards, my team comes together to talk things out. Then we'll pray, "God, we repent; forgive us for falling short; You know our hearts are right. Let everyone—especially the children—remember the *good* things that happened."

Most of the time, the next thing we know, we're receiving rave reviews from our hosts and the children. It's humbling and gratifying. The secret lies in keeping a right spirit. We brush ourselves off and go on to the next thing.

HOW TO MENTOR AND LIBERATE CHILDREN TO PRAY

Children can always be made free to pray. Here's what you need to keep in mind to release them:

Validate Their Personhood
They're people; little, yes, but still people. Praying validates them.

Acknowledge Their Spirituality
Once it's settled that children *are* spiritual beings, they will be perceived to be not only made "after the flesh, but after the Spirit." *Recognize and be convinced of their God-given right to be intercessors, beyond the traditional boundary of reciting sweet little prayers.*

What would you say to a nine-year-old boy—all boy—who weeps compassionately and comes out with a gem like this: "I hear the moans and groans of children being abused and orphaned. The Bible says I should cry with others who are crying. Right?"

Feeling the heart of Jesus, he cries with Him. As long and as fervently as wisdom allows in respect of his prayer anointing. Also, in respect, we have come to know by the Holy Spirit's prompting when it's time to say, "Thank you. Your tears rescued some children somewhere. It blessed Jesus to know you care about what He cares about." Then we celebrate. We laugh, sing, shout, dance, march, play—and the hosts of heaven join us.

Approve Their Mandate to Pray
Tell them who they are in Christ. Take them seriously. I tell them: "You are very important, mighty men and

women of God, full of the Holy Spirit and power. The Church needs you and your prayers. So does the world. God hears and answers your prayers just like He does mine. The same Spirit that raised Christ from the dead lives in you." Then, stand back and watch what God does in and through them.

Children who perhaps hadn't seemed that interested, are suddenly all agog about being "a house of prayer for all nations" (Isa. 56:7)! At the same time, children already tagged "intercessors," invariably take a quantum leap to pray even more powerfully.

Often, in a setting where children are coached and liberated to intercede, their prayers become so powerful so quickly, it leaves everyone in shock and awe, especially me.

Soon afterward, bewildered but enthralled parents and other spiritual leaders, stunned at what they now behold or confront, simply aren't sure what to do next. "Help! All our child wants to do is pray! Now what?" they'll exclaim.

"We don't even recognize our son!" one nonplused dad remarked. "For 12 years we've tried to get him out of his shell. Now, after only two hours with you, he's like this! What in the world happened in there?"

"In there" it was "like this."

His son, Sean, may not have known much more outside loving Jesus, being good and being cute. He tells us he prays for his daddy, mommy and sundry other family members including doggy and kitty. *Then, he's told that's great but there's much more. Right then he's* convinced that he's one of God's men for the hour. We pray. It puts him in touch with his spirit man. Without provocation, gut-level intercession gushes from very deep inside him for

CHILDREN ARE

REFRESHINGLY

NONRELIGIOUS.

THEY WILL

CREATE HAVOC

AT TIMES

WITH PIOUS

"CHURCHY"

ATTITUDES

ABOUT PRAYER.

abandoned children. Look out, world, the secret's out.

Be an Example
As I see it, every Christian is a prayer warrior. *Talk it, yes, but walk it, too.* In other words, *do it.* Long before my mother passed on her prayer mantle to me, I was groomed for it. I knew what she was by the way she lived. Children of intercessors certainly have an edge because they see prayer promoted and encouraged every day in the home.

Our CGPM children have observed their spiritual leaders, parents and/or grandparents in intercession and spiritual warfare. Their homes are houses of prayer for the nations. They hear us petition God for the lost. Why would one think it strange that they would want to cry for the lost with us? So we let them. The children see the priority of prayer in our lives, but we see the children's prayers as refreshingly honest, simple and forthright. Everyone gains.

Encourage, Encourage, Encourage
We wildly cheer them on with hoorays, high fives, "Y-YESs!" Be lavish with compliments. "Good job, B.J.!" Added hoopla for the simplest, stuttering, blubbering prayer as well as the most articulate, comes too, I think, from that "great cloud of witnesses" described in Hebrews 12:1.

Don't Make a Big Thing of the Small Stuff
Children are refreshingly nonreligious. They will create havoc at times with pious "churchy" attitudes about prayer. For example, as much as we explain Scripture, they still love to say, "Devil, go back to hell where you belong!" We don't get uptight about theology while they're praying. However, we'll review the Word again to instruct them for future prayers. "God overlooks things even in adult prayers," we tell them. I think He's big enough to tolerate it from all His *children*, including you and me. Don't you?

Listen, Listen, Listen to Their Spiritual Talk Patiently, Attentively
Children have insightful and startlingly discerning things to say. It's amazing how adults will go to great extents to open up a conversation about conventional, everyday affairs with children but often forget to listen to what is going deep inside a child's heart. Small gestures (like a child pointing to some part of God's creation), a small comment about God's daily goodness or even a question about why God made something a certain way is where our attentive listening may nurture a prayerful heart.

Converse with Them on a Spiritual Level
Ask questions of a spiritual nature. "What are you sensing? Seeing? Hearing from the Lord?" Ask them to pray for

your requests. Let them lead in prayer. After the initial shock from what you hear, you'll be so glad you did. And they'll be so glad you did, too.

I've had the guts occasionally to ask children, "How do you think I'm doing as your pastor's wife?" Or, living more dangerously, "Do you have a word from God for me?" (If you dare to do this, brace yourself for their stark honesty.) They'll have mind-boggling responses that may just trigger some healthy conviction. I know.

I love our church children, and they know it. I have these kinds of quality conversations with even the youngest ones. They're honest. Sensitive. Forthright. They have my full attention when they insist there's something of dire spiritual importance to say. There usually is. They hang on me, hug, kiss, grab, stroke and poke me. Could it be because they know I've got their spiritual number?

Invest in Their Spiritual Life: Money, Time and Attention
Adults understand the intrinsic value of children and the value in tending and nurturing their bodies and minds ever so carefully. But what about the spirit within each child? The world's attention is unmistakably fixed on children. Secular humanism, the New Age and others focus their efforts, spending billions of dollars in the process, to indoctrinate our children to "get in touch with their own spiritual powers and use human efforts to make a better world for themselves."

These signs of the times send a succinct, urgent message: Children are center front in the secular world controlled by an unholy spirit. To counterattack, I'd love to see families and churches direct more attention *and funds*—whatever it takes—to provide their children, *who are guided by the Holy Spirit*, with everything necessary to coach and liberate them to use their God-given spiritual authority in prayer.

"Train a child in the way he should go" (Prov. 22:6). Prayer is a given as one of the ways a child should go. You have the awesome responsibility—and privilege—to nurture, coach, equip and liberate young intercessors. Tell them they are "WorldShapers" for the new century and encourage them to pray for their families, churches, leaders, cities and nations. It takes time, creativity and sacrifice to cultivate a consistent and daily prayer life in a child's heart. No matter the obstacles, stay faithful.

The Internet: Use It for Prayer Meetings!
Children will find prayer partners they may never meet in person through the Internet. They'll chat and pray!

I have finally found my niche in the world of computers. I use this data mine for unleashing praying children! Our CGPMers are already sharing awesome prayer times. Our interactive website is pushing right through the congestion on this information superhighway. Enlisting your children in our CGPM or any of the fine children's prayer movements will get them connected. *We expect unsaved children who are surfing the net to log on to us and accept Jesus. Y-YES!* Using the Internet as a witness tool!

Create a Global Environment
To make children world-class prayer warriors, with a global mentality, bring the nations to them. Whether in the church or at home, it works easily. I was raised with

global thinkers and travelers. Flags, maps, pictures of missionaries, children from faraway countries, posters with relevant Scriptures were plastered everywhere. Plaques, too, about the world and prayer reminded me that "Prayer changes things" and that I should "Ask for the nations," and "Pray without ceasing." My childhood surroundings were conducive to whetting my desire for the world and for prayer.

Three beautiful, happy, busy children I know—all under 12—were already seasoned world-class intercessors at the time I visited their home. Why? How did this happen? Well, first, world maps covered the walls in every room with colored pins stuck in various places on it. Colorful plates, mugs, place mats, stickers—just about everything in sight—depicted the world. Unreached peoples statistics were tacked on a bulletin board; prayer requests were posted on the fridge door (even the magnets holding them were reminders). There were photos hung everywhere of children representing racial and ethnic groups. Bookcases and magazine racks were filled with books and magazines about the adventures of great people of God. Even their T-shirts were global in statement!

What a house of prayer! It seemed so easy to bring the world into their home; these wise parents simply created an environment to nurture what they knew God wanted for their children. *Osmosis*, I thought to myself. It's doable.

Instead of spending megadollars for a vacation, say, at Disney World, they redirect those funds and take their children on prayer journeys to foreign countries. The children find it the ultimate cool! So many are doing it these days. I'm warning you, they'll want to go again. Good-bye, Disney World; hello, worlds to conquer.

Respect Their Spirituality
Treating children's spirituality with respect, courtesy and recognition, mirrors Jesus. He neither hindered nor forbade them.

Trust Their Spirituality
They're not just cute; they're mighty prayer warriors!

Unleash Them to Pray!
With your blessing. Y-YES!

WILLING TO BE COACHED BY A CHILD

Incidentally, in my encounters with children, *I've* been coached by *them* more than a few times, too. But we won't go there. Oh, maybe just once. "Miss Esther, you stopped me before I *really* got through praying. God *really* didn't get to hear everything. I *really* need to finish."

My answer? "O-ooh, I'm *really* sorry. Forgive me. By all means, please finish." (I've never been guilty of doing *that* again, *really*.)

Thank God for special moments in the uphill fray. When a child sends me a note saying, "Miss Esther, you're doing a good job," I can live on it for another six months.

One note I'll always cherish came from Sean, six. He drew a picture of me—bright red dress, lips to match, very yellow hair, high heels—the works. The accompanying note read: "Miss Ester, your no dum blond!" (What a relief.)

Perhaps reappropriating some interests, some time and some funds, you'll carry things of eternal value to heaven. The idea itself carries with it the power and elements to forever change the course of many lives—yours, your family's, and a world full of others. It has been known to happen. Surprise! Surprise!

Adults who mentor children and who provide both an opportunity and an environment in which they can pray know something of God's heart for them.

Ponder this exclamation from a nine-year-old child: "Thanks for convincing my Dad and Mom that I've got the power just like they do!"

And consider this prayer prayed by children, unrehearsed or coached, in many a prayer workshop: "Dear Lord, please show my parents and my pastor how to teach me to be a mighty prayer warrior."

During a prayer meeting, Hannah, five, whispered to her mother, "These older people talk too much, Mommy. They don't really know how to pray. We should teach them."

I think the children teach us constantly. We just need to listen.

Notes

1. Carol Bellamy, *The State of the World's Children 1997* (New York: Oxford University Press, 1997), p. 4.
2. But there is another, different kind of laying on of hands that has to do with recognizing and ordaining church leadership. Timothy's apostolic church-planting gift was imparted through the laying on of hands by elders (see 1 Tim. 4:14). Timothy was warned not to be too hasty in installing new believers as leaders through the laying on of hands (see 1 Tim. 3:5,6; 5:22).

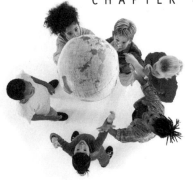

CHAPTER 4

ADVENTURES ON

the Prayground

Cool! Praying beats video games!

JEREMY, EIGHT

TEAMS TO GO: ON THE JOB

If you were to walk in on a children's prayer event already under way, you might find our team them along with workers and parents, all gung-ho, huddled around the 10/40 Window visual. You'd hear them interceding, calling out the names of nations; or they'd be in small groups focusing on numerous posters or banners, praying over specific issues; or stomping on a map of the world, as a prayer warrior, tearing down strongholds; or lying face down, weeping over the children of the world; or running their hands over a map of the world, declaring "Jesus is Lord!" over nations; or singing their intercession to lost children who are pictured on their posters, expressing in creative movement, "Jesus loves *you*, this we know, for the Bible tells us so . . . yes, Jesus loves *you*."

You might also just get in on a hilarious celebration or victory march or high praise. You'll want in on them all, but you're so overwhelmed, you don't know where to start! Happens every time, no kidding.

Perhaps you anticipated attending a regular church service and there you find the children, marching to the platform, singing the "House of Prayer March." This time, you and the whole church are feeling the electrifying effects of the anointing on the children. When a pastor allots us this privilege, it's probably one of the best favors he's ever done for himself. He's made room for a splendid finale by *unleashing his praying children and their prayers*. Vital to bringing the experience full circle. We complete our job in serving God, the pastor and his entire congregation, for under a powerful Spirit's anointing, the children "lead" in intercession, leaving everyone astounded and thoughtful.

"We're not just cute! We're mighty prayer warriors!" Using their *pray*ground voices, the children are allowed to point their fingers, just this once, at all the adults in the audience—even their pastors and parents—and literally bellow that declaration.

"Y-YES!" with fist and knee motions, the audience is instructed to shout back in affirmation, pointing their fingers, *"You're not just cute; you're mighty prayer warriors!"*

"Y-YES!" with fist and knee in position, the children roar in response.

Inevitably, it is followed by an exquisite moment of silence. I love that moment! Then, spontaneously, a celebration erupts, and the walls of man-made tradition come tumbling down!

The intercession and prayer warfare that follow bring even the least inclined people present right into the middle of things without even realizing what's happening to them—and everyone seated around them. I've seen pastors weep and celebrate openly. Presenting the things they had just learned, the children use the PRAYERTOOLS as warm-up and then get down to their job with a powerful anointing and with serious intent. Out of a seemingly cute thing, an explosive revelation occurs, known to revolutionize an entire church in an instant! Our team, having been invited by the pastor, has done its job. The moment of truth: unleashing the children and their prayer power, for such a time as this. Selah.

PRAYERTOOLS—FUN TO PRAY WITH!

Fabulous, anointed. They're grace gifts from God, developed in-house and hold, by God's hand, a before-and-after effect. Children who before may have been reluctant to pray, after using PRAYERTOOLS simply want to pray more, pray more! These helps are predestined to be persuasive! As one zealous young prayer warrior put it, "Cool! The more I get to pray, the more God gets to do!" The thought absolutely delights them.

The CGPM Prayer Gathering

Everyone is seated on a carpeted floor in breathless anticipation. All are dressed in T-shirts with "House of Prayer," "Catch the Vision—Get Global," or "It's time to pray not play, to weep not sleep," emblazoned with the CGPM logo on front, along with, of course, can't forget, the caps.

Our PRAYERTOOLS along with posters, banners, magazines, newspapers, maps, flags, musical instruments, etc. are in place, as if impatiently waiting for some action.

Green for "Go"!

David (CPGM International Director) shouts, "Okay everybody, repeat after me, good and loud!"

"We're on the *pray*ground!" (Everyone loves it! They catch on instantly.)

"We're on the *pray*ground!" they all shout back enthusiastically.

David continues, "The fabulous anointed PRAYERTOOLS are fun to pray with!" (They love this, too. They're fascinated.)

"The fabulous anointed PRAYERTOOLS are fun to pray with!" they respond even more excitedly.

Momentum is gaining. It's like electricity. The light is definitely green for "go"!

PREP TIME

Prayer Covering

Okay. Let's pray first. "Lord, we cover this place and all of us with the blood of Jesus. Thank You that we get to pray for the world! We're expecting lots of miracles! We're so excited about the fabulous time we're going to have; because of our prayers, children all over the world will come to Jesus!"

"Y-YES!" everyone responds enthusiastically with fist/knee motions.

Clean Hands; Pure Hearts

David continues, "Okay. Everybody, hold out your hands. They're now your spiritual hands" (Psalm 24 is explained).

Children repeat after him, "Lord, if I've done anything to make my hands dirty, please forgive me and wash them."

"Now, hands on your heart," he continues.

Children repeat: "God, if my heart isn't pure, make it pure right now. I want You to hear me when I pray and I must be anointed to fight the devil."

"Y-YES!" everyone shouts. Clapping and celebrating breaks out at this juncture. (I always feel during this exercise that greater works than just readying for prayer are accomplished.)

WorldShapers Asking for the Nations

There is good reason to call children WorldShapers. Our Children's Global Prayer Movement is up and running hard. Millions of mandated praying children worldwide are unquestionably shaping their generation.

In this exercise, after the children declare, "We're not just cute, we're mighty prayer warriors," the children repeat after David, "Revival will fill the earth. We're WorldShapers! God, Your Word says, 'Ask of me, and I will make the nations your inheritance,' (Ps. 2:8). We're going to just do it!"

Around the World on Our Knees.

Children repeat: "We will go on exciting adventures while we pray. By faith we can use our imaginations to see children in far-away lands coming to Jesus as we pray!" (see Heb. 11:1).

Today's godly children are prophets and see-ers. (see Joel 2:28). We encourage them to exercise all their spiritual senses. They feel Jesus' heart. They often speak things they hear that are beyond their own comprehension. Unaware, they inherently pray prophetically. Using their spirit eyes—"sanctified imaginations," we say—God shows them specific things that need their prayers or what answers are taking place as they pray by faith (substance and evidence), which children easily grasp and accept.

Intercession and Standing in the Gap

Even during our visual demonstration of these "big" words, intercession bursts forth (it's further described later on in this chapter).

Tearing Down Strongholds

Praying children confront the enemy with their sword, the Word of God.

For spiritual warfare, we explain the word "strongholds," making it two words ("strong holds"—i.e., false religions) and tell them they can take authority over strongholds in Jesus' name. The spirit realm is surprisingly clear to children.

The Declaration: The House of Prayer March

"Jesus said what the prophet Isaiah declared. "My house will be called a house of prayer for all nations" (Isa. 56:7, Matt. 21:13). With this rousing declaration, full marching band accompaniment and hand motions, the children march and sing, establishing and declaring their identity:

I am a house, a powerful house of prayer.
I am a house, a mighty house of prayer.
Jesus lives in me,
So I'm a house of prayer—
A powerful house of prayer—
A mighty house of prayer—
An awesome house of prayer
For all the nations!

Our prime example: "[Jesus] always lives to intercede for [us]" (Heb. 7:25).

Prayer Time with Doable PRAYERTOOLS

The GLOBALL is the size of a soccerball. This tool is soft, huggable, colorful and anointed! It is made of cloth and feels like a pillow, but is deliberately designed to be not perfect ("it's an imperfect world," we say). It's tossed around, sat on, laid on, slept with, cried on, sung with and (my favorite) fought over! The 10/40 Window, its focal point, is clearly outlined.

The Prayer Spinner

This game is so inviting! It's a user-friendly, brightly colored board game. Pie-shaped sections are labeled with global issues such as: Unity, the 10/40 Window, Abuse, Abortion, Violence, Unreached People, False Religions, and Laborers for the Harvest, etc. It draws children's attention away from themselves and gives them ideas for prayer, as they spin in anticipation of where the pointer will stop, to pray however the Holy Spirit leads. Once the spinning and praying starts, it's almost impossible to stop it!

Signs of the 10/40 Window Nations

Outfitted with these colorful, handheld signs, the children raise them high and declare with *pray*ground voices, "Jesus is Lord over Iraq!" and "Jesus is Lord over Afghanistan!" and "Jesus is Lord over Japan!" etc. Everyone responds with a rousing, "Y-YES!" Electrifying.

The "Window of the World" Song

It's Jesus' song with wonderful lyrics like "so many faces from all different places." Accompanied by slides of children from all over the world and expressed with creative movement, it's deeply touching, bringing with it a solemn quiet time. Then intercessions are poured out, going to heaven as incense, from genuine, caring young hearts; yes, even moanings and groanings. At times like these, I have often felt Jesus enter the room and walk gently, unseen, among us, listening.

The 10/40 Window Visual

Dramatic. Powerfully effective. Lights are dimmed. The large black window display held up by the children is closed. The story and statistics about the 10/40 Window are recited. With intensity, the Scripture is read, "See, darkness covers the earth . . . . Arise, shine, for your light has come!" (Isa. 60:1,2).

At that magnificent moment, the window is thrown open, flashlights turned on to shine on a brightly colored map of the nations, gold letters above reading "Shine, Jesus, Shine!" Everyone sings, changing the words to an outward message: "Fill *these* lands with the Father's glory . . . set *their* hearts on fire" while the names of the nations are called out to rise above the sound of the song.

Children have had visions or have seen pictures during this time: Buddhist statues toppling; Jesus appearing to Hindu children; angels, messengers to the heirs of salvation, visiting remote villages. Selah.

The WorldShaper Impression Ball

This little two-inch in diameter rubbery globe/ball stamped with "Catch the Vision" works wonders! It intrigues everyone.

Picture David, our international director, interacting with Bethany, six. David, I'm sure, has the original smiley face. His round brown eyes sparkle. His wonderful rapport is a gift from God. When he communicates with the children about prayer, everything is specta-a-a-cular and fanta-a-astic! With two children of his own, he knows how to make avid intercessors out of even the shyest or seemingly least interested ones.

Bethany was just that. She was shy, withdrawn, aloof. Purposely she would keep herself safely on the periphery, but not for long.

David said to her, "Hey, Bethany, you want to have some fun?"

Bethany says nothing, doesn't move, folds her arms. She simply looks toward the door.

David moves to bait her with that irresistible, anointed little ball.

"You can have this, Bethany. It feels kinda weird. Squishy. You can squeeze it and change its shape when you pray. You'll be making an "impression" on the world! Then we can call you our WorldShaper. Do you know what that means?

Bethany gives her head a soundly affirmative shake and grabs it out of David's hand. We're at that familiar not-sure-what-will-come-next point. She begins sobbing, squeezing hard that little ball, making her supplication known. She says, "Lord Jesus, I don't want women to have abortions and kill their babies anymore. Please help them to stop. Amen."

Everyone weeps with her—from the youngest to the oldest, the most tender to the toughest.

That's the transformation from Bethany the shy one to Bethany the intercessor in what seemed like just a nanosecond. Once again, it reminds us that this whole thing is God's idea, and He makes it happen. It's sobering.

OTHER SIMPLE, CREATIVE GOD IDEAS

Identity Praying

Same-age prayers. Same-name prayers. Everyone-else-who-has-to-wear-glasses prayers. Every-child-like-me-who-doesn't-have-a-daddy-at-home prayers, etc. This is limitless stuff. By now you've thought up dozens more yourself. The GLOBALL is tossed around with the shout of "Catch the vision—get global!"

Six-year-old Joshua catches it, hugs it close to his heart and prays, "Lord bless all the boys who are six, ah, girls, too. If they don't know Jesus, I want them to."

"Y-YES!" everyone agrees enthusiastically. Then he tosses it to another, shouting "Catch the vision—get global!" The exercise continues. It could go on forever.

Repeat-After-Me Prayers

Some children need just a bit more. Sometimes we run flat into a brick wall with children for one reason or another. Our PRAYER-TOOLS and simple prayer strategies—God ideas—really work.

For example, Kim, an oriental boy, five, shouts in newfound confidence: "I know the rest. In Jesus' name. A-a-a-a-MEN! Y-YES!" David patiently had helped Kim pray, a repeat-after-me-one-word-at-a-time kind.

David would say something like "Dear God," Kim: "Dear God," etc. I marvel at David's relentlessness. Then, suddenly, the grand finale bursts out of Kim's mouth and that was that!

"Y-YES!" the rest of us respond enthusiastically. Now not only David was smiling, but Kim was, too.

The 50/50 Prayer

This principle is transforming. Whatever the child's situation (physically challenged, unsaved parents, etc.), we first pray for him and then ask him to give half the prayer away as a gift to all the children who are just like him. Before we know it, he's praying—and weeping for them. No need to wonder why. In the process, we know he's receiving some personal healing, too.

Then we ask the children, "Can you imagine what it's like for children just like you who are in countries where there's war, no food, no education and no medical help? Put yourself in their shoes and let's pray for them."

Earnest pleas are made to the heavenly Father. Contemplative moments.

Standing in the Gap

Remember David's illustration? It's acted out with children representing God, a lost child and an intercessor between them. The intercessor hugs the sinner and takes him by the hand to introduce him to Jesus. Before you know it, all the children, whether they had shown interest or not, crowd together, hugging one another, interceding. They're softened; they'll weep. Hot, salty tears—tenderhearted—boys as well as girls. The Holy Spirit, in His time, comes to our aid to pray with us!

Just Like Jesus, Our Intercessor

"Do you know what Jesus is doing right now in heaven?" we often ask. (We get hilarious answers sometimes, but we won't go there.) After a few laughs, we get to the point. "He's interceding for us!" We want to do what he's doing. Intercession is just another kind of prayer. It's a pretty big word for some who've never heard it before. For others, on the other hand, it's old hat. But everyone repeats it after the leader syllable by syllable, "IN-TER-CES-SION." You can actually feel it stirring— unleashing them— as they speak it.

Here's are a few examples:

Akiel

He's only four years old.

David says, "Come on, Akiel, you can pray. You're a mighty prayer warrior."

Akiel replies, "No I'm not; I don't have a house of prayer T-shirt!"

"Gotcha." David throws a shirt on Akiel and the child is miraculously transformed into that mighty prayer warrior! Just like that. You can hardly stop him once he gets started!

Carlos

He's seven and off in a world of his own. David sits cross-legged on the floor with him, eye to eye. David says to him, "Carlos, do you know Jesus loves you and all the children in the world?"

"Uh-huh."

"Do you know that *millions* of them don't even know about Jesus?"

"Uh-huh."

"Well, do you think you should pray for them?"

"Huh-uh. Don't wanna. Ask him." (Carlos points to a veteran prayer warrior.)

David replies, "Aw, come on, Carlos, he's [the veteran] prayed enough. Show your stuff for Jesus! I'll help you, okay?

Suddenly, its a deal, GLOBALL included, and sealed with a high five Y-Yes! Prayer partners of an extraordinary kind, these two! Carlos's clean hands run with care over the 10/40 Window. He prays fervently from a pure heart—without David's help. Specta-a-a-cular!

Brian

"What in the world have you done to our child? You've gotten more out of him in half an hour than we have in 12 years!" Bryan's face is all aglow; but his parents register shock. Our answer to the question, which we're asked repeatedly, is always the same. "We told him that he can pray just as well as any adult, that God hears him and that he has the same Holy Spirit in him as you do. We called him a mighty prayer warrior. Then we let him pray. He's had such fun." Another 12-year-old, released and anointed to pray.

A veteran intercessor lies on the floor, hugging the GLOBALL. She is a see-er. "I see the children of Tibet. The Lord says they are hungry and helpless and that I must pray for them." She intercedes.

"Food is being dropped from airplanes right now!" declares another excitedly!

"Y-YES!" everyone yells gleefully.

Jeremy
He draws a "prayer picture"—the sun obscured almost fully by a black cloud. He says it means that some places are still very dark because Jesus hasn't been there. We all gather around, lay hands on his picture and pray for Jesus to shine through the darkness.

Jeremy then draws the answer! The brightest sun you ever saw! Everyone celebrates.

Katelin
She is our weeping reaper, naturally dramatic and creative. She kneels scrunched low, with her head to the floor as she prays. She also intercedes with the dance, twirling her way through the principalities and powers of darkness right into the heart of God. A wisp of a child, and beautiful, her intercessory prayer anointing dispels all doubt about children and prayer.

When given opportunity for their creative juices to flow, their ideas are often more effective than ours! We have great reverence for what God shows or says to them.

The Prayer Blanket

Imprinted with a map of the world. Even the remotest countries of the world, places where our praying children most likely will never go, are soon stained with the tears of young intercessors who are gripped with compassion for those who have never heard the name of Jesus. The children cover themselves with it, lie on it, weep in it. It's soft and cozy, but their intercessions are strong and mighty.

Speaking for the group, one 11-year-old mighty girl of God who obviously knows the Word, remarks, "I 'see' people of every tongue and tribe and nation changed forever. We'll get to see them for real someday in heaven, and we'll get to *know* them!"

"Y-YES!" the clamorous WorldShapers shout.

Then the blanket converts to a tent for some ecstatic celebration. I absolutely love it when children giggle and get downright rowdy at times like this. After all, we tell them over and over that a pretty wild party goes on in heaven when one soul is saved!

MORE HELP!

Posters
Made by the children, they depict issues that concern them, or they feature unreached people and information about them. Lots of faces on their posters.

Maps
Of everywhere. Children will lie on them and weep for the world. They'll run their hands lovingly over them and pray for the nations, states or cities.

Newspapers, Magazine Articles and Pictures, Too.

Music
Lots of music! For praise and worship, intercession and those stomp-on-the-devil warfare songs.

Missing Children
Have-you-seen-this-child? photographs.

Lapel Ribbons
In various colors representing current causes.

Lots of Pictures
Of churches, their pastors, leaders, workers; church bulletins; government officials; missionaries, teachers, schools.

Native Dress
Children attending a gathering will dress in the style of a country they want to represent for prayer. They really get into this one.

BOREDOM XED OUT

Our mighty prayer warriors never get bored. Just ask them. They kneel, jump, stomp, march or lie head down, flat on the floor. With eyes and hands fastened on our 10/40 Window PRAYER-TOOL or the posters they have made, they vie for a chance to pray! They sing, shout, praise and worship. They love to celebrate answers to prayer using tambourines, a variety of other rhythm instruments, flags and banners and doing "Jericho marches."

OUR MIGHTY

PRAYER

WARRIORS NEVER

GET BORED.

JUST ASK THEM.

THEY KNEEL,

JUMP, STOMP,

MARCH OR LIE

HEAD DOWN,

FLAT ON THE

FLOOR.

Ben's before-and-after picture of himself as he participated in a prayer gathering is typical of so many children. Before, he's looking very bored and slouchy, with hands in his pocket. After, he's jumping, all happy, holding up our GLOBALL. Best of all, his prayers indeed were heard and answered, and he knows it.

POWER RANGERS AND SPACE INVADERS OF A HIGHER KIND

"We're God's power rangers and space invaders!" announced a nine-year-old, with some accompanying animation. (These characters were "hot" at the time.) I didn't know the child, so I had to be discreet. "Well," I asked the adults in charge, "can we sanctify—clean up—these characters?" Does framing the word and putting the possessive "God's" in front of another word, idea or a toy make all the difference?

Can the children separate themselves from what these characters are and do and what we're doing?

After all, we're full of the power of the Holy Spirit, invading the heavenlies where spirits of darkness dwell, etc.

Children make comparisons. Sometimes we can use the current rage to teach a biblical truth and sometimes we can't. We have to look at the toys, board games, video games or TV characters that are "in" and decide with wisdom whether the characters can be made relevant to the children being mighty prayer warriors. If not, if we flat out reject the characters currently in vogue in the world of children, then we need to explain why. So whatever the current ever-changing rage is, at any time it surfaces, adults can determine (discern) if it might be eligible to be "sanctified."

WHEN TOOLS ARE
NO LONGER NEEDED

Settling into the intercessory prayer anointing, the children simply kneel, sit or lie face down, and cry out for extended periods for the world's children. Sometimes they're quiet, the stillness heavy with a profound air of supplication too deep for words.

Small groups mixing adults and children for intercession or using the "if two of you on earth agree" principle (Matt. 18:19) can become memorable experiences.

Bottom line—God only knows how busy He is, dispatching a host of His choice ministering angels to the ends of the earth, to the heirs of salvation—because praying children were unleashed to pray. Y-YES!

THROUGH THE
EYES OF A
Child

CHAPTER 5

CHILDREN'S PRAYERS,

Simply Profound

I will pour out my Spirit on all people. Your sons and daughters will prophesy.

JOEL 2:28

WHAT CHILDREN LOVE TO PRAY

Have you wondered what issues and people are important to children when they pray? Have you ever taken the time to listen carefully to the natural outcry of petition that children offer to God in prayer? If you are a parent, teacher or Sunday School helper who wants to encourage children to grow in supplication and petition before the Lord, then the first task is to *listen to the children*. What's important to the hearts of the little ones whom Jesus cherishes?

As adults, we should never look down upon children and their words to us, but we should weigh everything in light of

Scripture. When children encourage and prod us in the Lord's work, we have to measure their words against the Lord's Word. If their words are sound in biblical principle, then we should take to heart what is being shared to us (see 1 Thess. 5:19-21).

Today's godly children and prayer are inseparable, hence "Prayers are us!" is a familiar phrase among the children we work with. Here's a snapshot of the world of these children's prayers—prayers that are genuine and very powerful in the sight of God.

Children Desire Peace Among Their Spiritual Leaders
Prayer: Dear Lord, let pastors know You'll do great things when their leaders stop arguing (for peace among Christians see Ps. 133; Gal. 5:13-15).
Result: One pastor readily admitted it to be true. Soon after, he told us he had fasted and prayed and God gave him a plan to reorganize his leadership.

Children Understand Godly Priorities
Prayer: Pastor, as I was praying for you, the Lord said to tell you: "You're too busy with your building program." He says to take care of the building inside you, and He'll take care of your church building (for setting our priorities correctly in Christ see Ps. 127:1,2; Rev. 2:1-5).
Result: The pastor said he felt as if he were near a nervous collapse. But the moment the child touched him, his body fell gently to the floor where he lay quietly for quite a long while. He rose totally renewed.

Children Show Adults What Childlike Reliance Means
Prayer: Pastor, when I laid my hand on you to pray, God told me: "You're getting your sermons from your own

head" and He wants you to get them from Him (for reliance on God see Prov. 3:5,6; Jer. 17:5-8).

Result: The pastor publicly repented of the error of his ways and then asked his congregation to forgive him.

Children have a beautiful understanding about the spiritual issues surrounding and affecting their churches and other Christians, but they also have a clear sense of what's affecting society as a whole.

We asked a group of 100 children under 10 who were ready and waiting to pray what was on their hearts. Here are the issues that concerned them about their city:

• racism	• gambling	• street violence
• thefts	• mafia	• gangs
• smoking	• mocking	• garbage piles
• kidnapping	• drive-by shootings	• murder
• drugs	• school bombings	• alcoholism
• TV/video violence	• sex ouside marriage	• children having children
• prostitution	• occult sacrifices	• vampire cult
• divorce	• the homeless	• abandonment
• child abuse	• poison candy	• foster children

Children will fervently pray about all these matters, if we release them to intercede and petition at home and in church.

Heavenly Prayers and Prophecies for Pastors

Often children's prayers are short and to the point. I remember an occasion involving about 50 pastors. These godly men lay prostrate, weeping for their city. They had mobilized about 40 children there for a simultaneous prayer gathering in another room. But God had another plan. To this day I don't know how it happened, but while the children were praying, they simultaneously crashed the adult goings-on, rushed to the pastors and began ministering to them. No one could interfere.

Children laid down close beside these pastors, some actually on top of them, weeping, hugging and touching them tenderly. Travail was upon the children for the Shepherds. Real, unadulterated, Holy Ghost anointed travail. A spirit of supplication. The pastors couldn't move. What they received from the children's prayers, only heaven knows. Here in capsuled form is what the children prayed and prophesied that night. Really.

- Dear God, keep these pastors pure. I want You to please keep them safe.
- Dear Lord, please help them to tell the truth.
- Dear Jesus, I want these pastors to love their wives and families and churches.
- Please don't let people treat them bad unless they treat people bad.
- Dear Jesus, would You please help these pastors. They have the hardest job in town.
- Lord, keep them healthy; make them eat right and exercise, so they can live long.
- Dear God, make sure they read the Bible and pray, so they won't sin.
- Jesus, I want them to love You more every day; some don't love You like they used to.
- I want You to tell them how much You love them.
- God, I want my pastor to smile and laugh more.

- Dear God, if any of these pastors have some secrets and if they're doing stuff they shouldn't be doing, please help them stop—right now!
- Devil, in Jesus name, you and all your demons, just GO! You can't bug these pastors anymore.
- You'll have some big stuff going on, but never mind, God will show you what to do about it.
- Tell all your people they'd better brace themselves; God is about to visit your church.
- Sorry, Pastor, but you're not thinking big enough. God wants your new building to be much bigger.

Although everyone present was in reverential awe, I think I was awed the most. I usually am. And, as always, the most humbled, too.

CHILDREN ARE PROPHETS HARD TO IGNORE

"Stay under the anointing, so you don't mess up!" That was the haunting admonition from a nine-year-old prophet. The boy got the last word and it exploded the atmosphere where nearly 500 people had assembled for our first intergenerational churchwide gathering.

A dozen or so pastors and leaders were seated on the platform of the church. Just as we were about to close a powerful and exhilarating morning of interaction in intercession, the prophet, acting just like Joel of old said he would, suddenly turned directly to the pastors, pointed a fiery finger at them and delivered, unhesitatingly, this shocking admonition.

Tangible silence fell. Slowly, the pastors began weeping. Some dropped to their knees, repenting. The congregation broke into quite a raucous celebration beholding God's awesome work-ings. But their euphoria came to a screeching halt when this hot prophet pointed that fiery finger at them and bellowed, "And that means you, too!" Dead silence again. Not a soul in the place could escape him—or God.

Children Speak to Pastors

The Sunday morning clock-watchers were glued to their seats long after their traditional noon (on the dot) dismissal. Their pastor, who had told us he had not involved the children all that much in spiritual ministry, found himself flat on his back on the platform for two hours while they prayed and prophe-sied over him. It was a divine five-and-a-half-hour blockbuster prayer meeting (by "blockbuster," I mean that it busted blocks . . . religious blocks, intellectual blocks, blocks of accepted man-made traditions and teachings, blocks of opin-ions and judgments about what praying children of all cul-tures can or cannot, should or should not do). Savor the *good news*. Y-YES!

A fax from the pastor awaited us upon arriving home. It was a copy of a memo he had circulated to his department heads the very next morning, which read:

> This is to inform you that from today on, I expect children
> to be included in every department of church ministry.

I must confess that I often wave that treasured piece of paper heavenward and cry, "Oh, God, please multiply this miracle like Jesus did the bread and fish!" Pastors, if you read me, a little help from you wouldn't hurt.

Children Encourage Adults to Pray

Children are endearing in their capacity to provoke us and encourage us to pray. Consider Lacey, two, who would tug at my sleeve with this admonition every time she saw me! "Pray more, Etter. Pray more!" That's a hard invitation to turn down.

Lacey's genuine desire that I diligently pray is so compelling that I've instructed adults in conferences and churches around the world to do this: Tug on your own sleeve or the sleeve of someone nearby and say, "Pray more (name of person). Pray more!" Believe me, this really works wonders! I dare you to try it on yourself.

One five-year-old boy made the point about the importance of prayer when he said, "Daddy, if Jesus prays all the time, shouldn't we?" The child's remark came from his simple, profound logic. It was a statement rather than a question. This is one to ponder. Perhaps it should be plastered on church marquees around the world or printed in their bulletins. It could make for a great intro in flyers promoting prayer conferences, too.

Children are refreshingly direct with adults. Once at a National Day of Prayer event in Washington, DC, I mobilized 40 children to pray. While on the mall, a TV network newscaster listened to the children pray and began to interview them. The reporter said rather incredulously, "No mincing words with these children. Their prayers cut right to the core."

In response to her I said, "Yes, they say it like it is, and they pray it like it is, too."

Events as I've just described are a wonderful reminder for me how children are ready assets at home, in church and in the city. All we need to do is ask them to pray. Watch what happens.

CHILDREN ARE PACESETTERS

Parents all over the world tell us that their children's intercessory prayer life has changed their home, lifestyle, church and even plans for the future. One family wrote:

> After our daughter's GCOWE '95 prayer experience, our entire family was launched into a new dimension of prayer ministry. We also allowed her to change schools after she explained that the vision of the school she was attending was too small now and she simply didn't fit in there anymore.

There are many reasons that draw children to pray and intercede for others. One of the most compelling was a letter I received from Lisa, 11 (I've changed her name because of the sensitive nature of the material). Her sincere heart and her wisdom to petition God in prayer exhorted my own heart to pray.

Dear Miss Esther and the CGPM,

You said we could send you our prayer requests. This is a very important one. My mother said it was okay for me to write. She's helping me. I'm very sad about this.

A month ago, my father was put out of his church (he was a pastor) because he was committing adultery. Everyone was pretty upset. Especially my mom and my brother. The church people were upset the most. I cried myself to sleep for a whole week. Then I decided to do something you taught me. I began to pray about it. I felt a little better. Then I decided to do something else. I got all my church friends together and we're having prayer meetings for the church and for my dad. I'm leading it. It has helped me!

Miss Esther, would you please pray for us and ask your

CGPM to pray for us, too? But don't use my name. I don't want to embarrass my dad. Thank you.

Love,
Lisa

After reading this letter, it was *my* turn to cry for a week. But I also practiced what I had taught Lisa to do. I prayed about it and "felt a little better." The CGPM took it to the Lord, but it lingers in my mind. I think it will, forever. I never heard from Lisa again.

Children's Prayers Show GLOBALL Caring

Children pray as powerfully as adults, particularly for the 10/40 Window nations. Six-year-olds weep for hours in intercession for their counterparts in Tibet, Iran, China and India—where the children have almost no reasonable chance to hear the gospel of Jesus Christ in their lifetime.

"Our girls intercede with the GLOBALL for countries and islands, that children living there will know Jesus and receive Bibles," a dad and mom said. "Then our five-year-old will go into warfare against Satan—powerful but simple! We pray together as a family with excitement and anticipation."

To intercede and engage in spiritual warfare gives children ultimate satisfaction in knowing they can take authority in the name of Jesus over matters that gravely concern them. It gives them such joy. They revel. They love to celebrate when they sense a breakthrough. Like being propelled, ecstatic in knowing God hears and answers them. Most of the time, believe me, it's difficult to shut them down! No doubt. They are freed to shout their personal "Hosanna, God save us!" (see Matt. 21:9) for their own generation.

Children's Prayers Are Revealing

Under the intercessory prayer anointing, children see amazingly accurate scenes.

> During Desert Storm, as we were praying at home, the children felt led to pray for the American servicemen there. The Lord gave our daughter a movie-type vision. "I see the inside a building in the desert; it's all underground." (She described everything there.) "In one room I see a missile. They can't make it work properly; we must pray that they won't." (This is prior to the media mention of underground bunkers.) "I see an American plane. It has been hit and it's coming down. The pilot is okay. He's getting out of the plane but he needs somewhere to hide. Enemy troops are not far away. An American plane is looking for him; we must pray that it will come further and find him." We prayed until the burden lifted from her.

It was amazing to later read, in a well-known magazine, the correlating testimony of the pilot who was shot down.

In another testimony a parent said:

> My daughter, Rachel, grabbed some paper and began to draw. I asked her what she was doing several times, but she didn't hear me. She carried on drawing. I asked her what it was and she didn't know. When she had finished, she had drawn an underground complex with various rooms. She drew the disguised watch places and the above-ground camouflages. We prayed till we felt God intervene for whatever it meant.

Children's Prayers Are Healing

One parent describes how her child prayed for healing in the most unusual of places—a restaurant. Here's what happened:

> When she was three years old, our daughter, Julie, would minister healing by laying hands on people and saying, "Jesus, make them better." While in a restaurant, she laid hands on a young lady having a migraine headache. She had a life history of migraines. The pain left instantly and she has never had another migraine since. This miracle caused forks to be dropped and it raised the attention of everyone in the restaurant.

There is a dynamic scriptural principle being employed when children pray for others so that they too may be healed and comfort others through prayer with the comfort they have received from God (see 2 Cor. 1:3-5).

When children pray on their knees for others around the world, sometimes on their faces, they are undertaking an exciting prayer journey. They stop to sightsee in the needy places on their hearts to heal and comfort others and tell them about Jesus' love. Extraordinary tales of their prayer treks let us know that God has piloted them all the way.

Children's Prayers Are Sometimes Humorous

Praying children—and their prayers—can give us superb comic relief that one couldn't conjure up in a 100 years. Children are such master hams. The funniest thing is that they can provide great laughs without even knowing it. The best thing is that they can laugh at themselves.

"DE-DUS IS
WO-ORD OBER
A HO WO-O-RD!"
THIS THREE-
YEAR-OLD'S
RENDITION
MUST HAVE
DELIGHTED
JESUS.

I know intercession is a serious matter. Interacting with the children has been my greatest encouragement to continue. Jesus said that His yoke is easy and His burden is light (see Matt. 11:30). Adult intercessors can carry an undue heaviness. *It would do us good to let the children lead us to a place of joy in the house of the Lord* (see Isa. 56:7). If more of us would be more childlike in our approach to the matter of intercession, perhaps a lot more of us would be a lot less wary—or afraid—of it.

Being with children, I'm constantly reminded how they take things so literally. We were singing, "Red, brown, yellow, black and white—Jesus loves the little children of the world" during a time where we'd been dealing with racism and prejudice. Our leader then asked Jimmy, five, "Would you please pray for all the colors?"

Jimmy took a deep breath and commenced thoughtfully: "Dear God, please bless blue; it's nice but I like gre-e-n. Thank you God, for girls' colors like pink and orange. In Je . . . oh, yeah, and all the colors in that song, too. In Jesus' name, Amen."

"Y-YES!" everyone answered respectfully. After which, we roared with laughter (I told them everyone in heaven loves to laugh).

Delightful stories come from "Jesus is Lord" declaration over the nations. My favorite is "De-dus is Wo-ord ober a ho wo-o-rd!" This three-year-old's rendition must have delighted Jesus, especially since He's grieved so much to hear His name profaned, albeit so articulately. To say nothing of the strongholds all over the world that crumbled at this big little warrior's command. It may have toppled an antichrist government. Who knows? "De-dus." Sometimes I feel like using it myself.

MY CHILDHOOD PRAYERS ANSWERED

I know God hears every prayer children petition. I also know He *answers* the prayers of children, from a magnificent event that happened in my own childhood.

Daisy was nine. I was four. But the memory is stark. All I knew was that my big sister couldn't move her arms or legs, and I was scared.

"Mr. and Mrs. Shabaz," the doctor's voice quivered, "your daughter is paralyzed. She will never walk again."

Undaunted, Mr. and Mrs. Shabaz, knowing instinctively what to do next, gathered their son and four daughters together and called the pastor in. What came to pass was the most vigorous prayer meeting conceivable.

Nothing changed immediately. Our house was quarantined and I was taken, frightened and confused, to stay with an aunt. Nonetheless, we were all kept in perpetual prayer mode. Our church went into a season of fasting and prayer. After a few months, our

Sunday School superintendent called. He told us that the entire church was joining Daisy's Sunday School class of nine-year-olds and would spend the day praying for a miracle.

Enter Jesus the healer!

At some miraculous moment during that sweet hour of prayer, Daisy's arms and legs suddenly began flailing. She was jubilant. "Mommy, Daddy," she shouted, "come quick! Look! I'm healed!" She could move all her limbs.

I will always consider this event my ultimate answer to prayer, my supreme coup d'état over the devil. What happened to Daisy is a lifelong memory that has proven to be a vital source of assurance. It rescues my faith whenever it wavers. Symbolically, it convinces me again and again that prayer can move everything, even mountains, according to the Word.

This event was embodied in the predestined curriculum of my childhood and worked together to stamp a guarantee in my tender young heart that God hears and answers children's prayers.

The accounts of children praying for families, parents, pastors, teachers and churches are innumerable. The simply profound prayers of children are powerful. Who can tell what has been changed, intercepted, accomplished! Whatever; one thing I do know: It's headline-making *good news!*

CHAPTER 6

PRAYING CHILDREN,

Ready Assets

And the grace of God was upon him.
Jesus grew in wisdom and stature, and in favor with God and men.

LUKE 2:40,52

FIXING THINGS AROUND THE WORLD

Children are wonderful ready assets through whom come profound truths and miracles. Much of what you will read in this chapter are their words, their heart, their desire to pray. You will be amazed at all the things they can cover.

I remember a conversation I had with an educator from Russia shortly after the Berlin Wall had come down. After listening intently to our vision, his response went something like this:

Mrs. Ilnisky, what you are doing provides the best psychological cure for the children in places like Russia where there has been bondage and isolation from the world. For our children to realize there are children in need all over the world and then to be taught to pray for them will be a great part of their own healing. It will be a critical for them and will give them a whole new outlook on life.

Children have prayer treks where God moves their hearts to pray for peoples and nations around the world. Just knowing that God cherishes their prayers for other communities and countries literally transforms children. They talk to God more often; their compassion is nurtured and they become very ready assets to a very sick world.

Ready Assets in Spiritual Warfare

In Argentina, I had my first experience with praying children outside the United States. In one church, 200 children (ages 3 to 12) are directing children's services, interceding for others to know the Lord, and prayer walking through their neighborhoods. There are reports of many spiritual strongholds breaking through the intercession of these young ready assets.

A young prayer warrior once, while lying facedown on a map of the United States, declared, "I see demons leaving violent men!" We had been in prayer warfare against violence and abuse in America. Then this young ready warrior, as I see it, began a process of deliverance in men, perhaps saving some from committing this shameful offense ever again.

I often ask the children after an active session on the *pray*-ground, "How do you feel?" Their one-word answers are enough for

me! "Good!" "Peaceful!" "Fantastic!"
"Happy!" "Great!"

How did you like it? It takes only one one-word answer to say it for all of them. *"Cool!"*

Ready Assets in Seeing the World Come to Jesus

Michael, 15, once prayed, "Dear God, this world's a mess; please come and fix it." This prayer was spoken in about 10 seconds, includ-ing a sigh between sentences—voila! One could pray eloquently all night and hardly do better. Direct and to the point. I have a feeling that incalculable things on the planet readily got fixed. Quite a ready asset, wouldn't you say?

Yet children often pray about things unseen, things not in their immediate view, but definitely seen by their heart.

"I'm weeping for the children of Tibet," explained Lindsay, six, as she hugged the GLOBALL in her bedroom. "God told me they were homeless and helpless. I hear them crying." A ready asset—perhaps making a way through her petitions for help to arrive?

"DEAR GOD, THIS WORLD'S A MESS; PLEASE COME AND FIX IT."

MICHAEL

Tai, seven, submitted his concept of how to raise up praying children around the world. "You do it, I watch. I do it, you watch. We do it together. You do it with someone else. I do it with someone else. They do it with someone else. Then, all the someone elses fill the whole world."

"Help the president of the United States to not obey Satan but to obey You, God." T.J. and Hannah ganged up to pray this one. How's that for two ready assets petitioning God on behalf of a nation's leader?

"The 10/40 Window is filled with angels! Some of them are headed right now for Hindu children to tell them about Jesus!" declared Ben, eight, excitedly. "And they're going to their parents to tell them to worship Jesus. Doesn't God's Word say He'd send angels to people who will be saved because we pray?"

"Y-YES!" everybody yells, with fist and leg motions.

Ready assets, with a little help from angels.

Ready Assets in Bringing About Miracles Seen and Unseen

It takes faith to grasp this one. Rebecca, 10, and her parents were vacationing for the weekend—they thought. It was Saturday evening when suddenly Rebecca announced, "I can't stay here anymore. God told me some people are in danger and I have to go home and pray. Now!" Wise parents, discerning the urgency in her voice and the intercessory prayer anointing which had come upon her, promptly packed up and went home. Only eternity will reveal what that call to prayer accomplished. I think Rebecca will always be willing to drop everything to be a ready asset.

I shared this account with a person who quickly let me know I was responsible for ruining a child's fun by teaching them to be on the alert to pray. I'm not sure where it came from; but I said,

"Wait a minute. Don't be too hasty to pass judgment; maybe, just maybe, *you* were in danger and she prayed you out of it. Maybe that's why you're still here." Who knows?

Don't underestimate the power that children's prayers have on the world. In Malaysia it was reported that 50 children fasted and prayed over the Japanese encephalitis virus that was killing many men who ran pig farms and who were the sole breadwinners for their families. The children's prayers were stirring and many children had visions. One saw an angel blessing the nation. After that there was a sharp drop in the mortality rate due to the disease.

The point is: Godly children are ready assets that shape the world through their prayers and we only see the very tip of how their petitions transform individuals, communities and entire nations.

Praying Births Ready Assets

Ready assets. They've been readied by God to pray, from the foundations of the earth. Recognize them. Take full advantage of their prayer power. Let their abounding, uncontaminated faith be unleashed on the impossible, and just watch what happens. Tap into these amazingly fixed and ready assets. It's smart. Y-YES!

Tamara, eight, once gave a prophecy that I think is very crucial for adults. She declared: "'Prayer is very important! Children are a big part of prayer. They are and will be a very special part of My end-time plan,' says God!" I take serious note of these words: "We get to pray!" Yes, children want to pray. They *love* to pray. Today's godly children are born to pray. God has put the desire in them. I know. I have myriad dazzling proofs. By the time this book goes to print, I will have a never-ending etcetera of glorious accounts that could fill a book of its own.

These remarkable ready assets, mostly 12 and under, don't know the art of taking literary license. They simply await instruction; then, without preambles, analyses or discourses, they promptly get to the point, combining every necessary ingredient—purity, faith, trust, hope, belief, expectation—for getting answers from God.

Kathryn Snider, CGPM rep on the island of Jamaica, understands how children are God's ready assets! She reported how the children's prayer ministry team was powerful and was well received at Emmanuel Church in Mandeville, Jamaica. "As the children prayed, God showed me that their prayers would enable Him to do what He wanted to do in people's lives."

And what did the children say? "It was great!" "It was fun!" "I want to do this again and again!"

But the best news is how prayer changes the lives of the children. One report I received from Java said it perfectly: "New life is most obvious among our children who were once unmanageable and rebellious and now radically converted. Parents tell us they don't recognize their children. No more abusive language. Some have started prayer meetings in their schools."

That's a picture of radically changed ready assets radically changing the world.

CHAPTER 7

PRAYING CHILDREN EQUAL

Praying Adults

To our beloved Esther, Your calling is the best. Pray—there is no other way but to trust and obey. Depend on the Holy Spirit to know what to say. We pray without ceasing day and night for God to keep you safe and secure by His heavenly light. Because He promised a crown full of stars as reward, Beloved, keep on praying to Christ, our Lord.

YOUR LOVING MOTHER AND FATHER

CHILDHOOD LEGACIES

There is no doubt in my mind that praying as a child leads to praying as an adult. Examples of adults who fervently pray inspire children to do the same as they enter adulthood. My life is a reflection of that principle. The two greatest examples of prayer in my life were my mother and father.

Mother's Place of Prayer

Karl Barth, a Swiss theologian of the early twentieth century, once said that Christians with God's heart for the world pray with the Bible in one hand and a newspaper in the other.

In that case, my mother certainly knew God's heart. Daily she could be found in her bedroom-turned-prayer room/battle station—amid piles of magazines, maps, pictures and newspapers, petitioning God for, well, everything.

From the time I was three we prayed together for the world. I remember crawling all over those prayer requests strewn on the floor, absorbing my mother's prayers. When my four older siblings were off to their school, I was in mine, a school of prayer, with my teacher/mentor, my mother. A little lady and her little girl, fondly called "Estherbaby." Two giant prayer warriors.

As Mother's exquisite voice cried out for worlds beyond her human reach, my little voice would cry out, too. Those compassionate tears dropping on her papers, and on me at times, made me cry, too. Her joyful praise was contagious. Her dancing heart rejoiced in what her spirit's perfect vision saw in response to her passionate petitions. My little feet then would dance about. She was my example. I did everything she did. Best of all, she made me feel like a very important prayer partner!

Mother led our church's Ladies Prayer Meeting. Every Wednesday without fail, she'd whisk me, just a preschooler, off with her to that all-important meeting. Etched on my heart forever are those numberless hours in the presence of faithful prayer-warrior women who, *while in the process of changing the world, were shaping my future.*

Excerpts from Mother's legacy and from gems found written in her Bible:

• I will be watching and waiting for you, dear family, to

meet me in heaven. I will be expecting you! Let Him have His way in your life, and lean on His everlasting arms. Of this world's goods I have very little, but I leave with you the legacy of love. I commit you to the Lord who will guide you with His light and love to your heavenly home.

- If some problem disturbs your sleep, don't count sheep—talk to the Shepherd.
- Don't be afraid to go to God in prayer. He will never say "Come back when I am not so busy." But He might say, "You gotta be kidding!"

Grasping Hold of Father's Faith

My father was a jolly, optimistic man of great faith despite the fact that he had survived the ravages of the first World War and religious persecution in the Middle East. Along with the sadness of seeing many loved ones martyred and being forced from his homeland, was the loss of his identity. An articulate, well-schooled man, tutored by Presbyterian missionaries, he had been the pastor of a thriving church and the esteemed mayor of his village.

One would never have imagined him to be a refugee from the Old Country, narrowly escaping death during the persecution of Christians, which took the lives of many in his own flock. Working with his hands as a common laborer in the grimy steel mills of Gary, Indiana, could not quench his indomitable spirit nor dim the ever-present twinkle in his soft brown eyes.

His "prayer gallery" accommodated dozens of photographs displayed on a coffee table set in a tiny walk-in closet! His daily routine in that place started with cheerfully shouting while looking at the pictures, "Good morning, everybody!" Then he'd pray boisterously over each one. His finale was to loudly invoke blessings on all those favored by God to have their pictures grace that sacred table! As a child, it fascinated me. I loved being in there with him. It was sheer fun. It housed, providentially for me, a unique, enchanting school of prayer.

Father had the soul of a poet. He insisted that his poetry, translated from his native language just for me, would still rhyme. Like the poem which began this chapter. Simple and sweet, yet commanding.

Grandmother's Chair

"Dayah," we lovingly called her. This dynamite woman of God, though tiny in stature, held a giant presence in our household. I see her sitting cross-legged in her prayer chair, from where she talked to Almighty God three times a day. Every day. Her voice matched her presence. That chair, to me, is the "conversation piece" of all time. An illustrated lesson in yet another school of prayer.

THE LESSONS OF HERITAGE

With such great examples in my own life, it is not surprising to me how true my husband's remark was when he said, "Remember, Esther, these children are going to grow up. Try to see them into the future, what they will become, partly because of your influence."

My husband's words, spoken to me in the earlier days of my journey/joyride, always kick back at the right times, in one form or another. I'll hear either from or about my children (all the intercessors) now turned teenagers. The 12-year-olds I started with are 17 and over at the writing of this book. Oh, yes, have they *ever* grown up! My husband was so right.

WORLDSHAPERS BORN FROM CHILDREN

The prayer mandate of these children has grown up, too. You know how it's said that children today grow bigger than their parents? It could apply with regard to their prayer life, too. Think about it. A mother put it this way: "Esther, I was never the prayer warrior my son is when I was his age. I'm not even where he's at now. He's way ahead."

Those children-turned-teens who've continued to be mentored and encouraged to wear this mantle of intercession, this spirit of supplication, to be WorldShapers, are making their mark in Christendom. They have pioneered youth prayer movements that are going full blast. They're warriors, full of the Spirit's power, directing their endless energy to battling Satan's hold on their generation. Their unleashed prayer power is invading principalities and powers of darkness. They're loud about it. Tough, too. Their voice in their corner of the culture is literally erupting in the X and Y generations—WorldShapers—plowing the route in the years between then and now.

These young people are rising as acknowledged and viable leaders of prayer ministries in their churches and by the leadership of their National Prayer Networks as well as the Worldwide Prayer Movement. They're making their mark on Christendom. I'm told they can be quite a challenge to their parents and pastors. No doubt.

If it's a problem, it's a good one! A pastor friend remarked laughingly, "Say, Esther, don't do me any more favors. My young people are banging on my office door and they're in my face every chance they get, demanding more time and space for prayer meetings. They're also doing a number on my children's workers to get the children praying, too." He paused and then continued, "But I'll have to admit; their intercession is working miracles in the church."

I *love* those true confessions.

Growing Up to Slay Spiritual Giants

It happened while our CGPM children participated in the United States National Day of Prayer in Washington, DC, held on the steps of the Capitol. Thirty children! Some had been in solid intercession and prayer warfare for three days.

Now, as their powerful prayers were unleashed, I saw the children in a vision, as footprints indelibly engraved forever into the cement. The wind took their prayers echoing through the offices and corridors of the complex of buildings that house the nation's government. Then the vision became prophetic. I saw these children as adults, again standing in the same place, this time as leaders in government, openly taking their stand, interceding for a spiritual awakening in their nation.

I recently visited in the home of one of my former 12-year-old prayer warriors. She lives in a two-story house and the young lady's bedroom is upstairs. The "upper room," indeed. This time it was a group of young people pounding the gates of hell in some pretty fierce warfare for their nation (shades of my mother's war room).

RANDOM KALEIDOSCOPE VIEWS OF THEIR PRESENT AND FUTURE

There is joy in my heart over watching young people wrestle in prayer against spiritual strongholds, but there is also joy in seeing them grow in wisdom in passionately interceding for others through prayer. Perhaps you're curious to know how prayer is seen in their eyes over time. Here's what a few of my prayer champions had to say:

Annie

Since being exposed to global prayer, I have a global perspective on everything. I feel set apart (I feel as if I were ordained in Korea in 1995), given permission to go out and do. I've been going and doing ever since. I've asked God, *Why am I so different?* Yes, I've had some rejection, but I've dealt with it. I feel called to the leaders of the world. I want to network/plant churches around the world. Then have a production company to produce dramas, TV, radio, plays, etc. to distribute throughout the network of churches.

Daniel

In my praying experiences as a child, I was rough around the edges. Then God began refining me. An authority was imparted that has gotten stronger over the years. I've been to Taiwan and Nepal, speaking and praying there. Also to Columbia five or six times—prayed over youth and children. Then we all prayed over the adults.

My high school is where all the druggies, the gang members and alcoholics go. There are fights, violence and blood. Many atheists and backsliders. I've shared my witness. Not once have I ever been ridiculed. I've been put on a course I'll continue all my life. Not sure of everything ahead, but I know it's for full-time ministry.

"GLOBAL PRAYER

CHANGED

MY LIFE

DRASTICALLY.

THE SKY IS

THE LIMIT

CONCERNING

MY FUTURE."

SHANNON

Marcus
My first experiences in global praying got me plugged into the whole world. It basically got me fired up for God. Gave me my missions perspective. I've been to China, Africa and Brazil. God spoke to me about Brazil while I was in Korea. My call to missions came there. He's working out the process.

Shannon
Global prayer changed my life drastically. I've been to Mexico to minister to the children. The sky is the limit concerning my future. I want to do all for God.

I've kept track of other World-Shapers, too. Their stories show the same wonderful commitment to intercede for family members, friends, churches and nations.

Sarah and Japheth
Both are traveling with their parents teaching children to pray. Their leadership qualities will work to send them off on their own someday.

Nicole
She now has a prayer ministry of her own among the youth of her state. Young people from surrounding states are attending. Her prayer ministry is recognized by spiritual leaders as one of the most powerful avenues of prayer available to young people.

She has a grave concern for her nation and is mobilizing these youth to come together to intercede for it. As Nicole continues on this path, she looks toward a growing prayer ministry that will reach around the world.

Richard
He continues to travel in the intercessory prayer ministry.

Hayden
He honestly and openly shares his own struggles with rebellion, lust, impure thoughts, swearing and selfishness, and tells how to overcome these spiritual struggles.

Ryan
He has big plans. He is a big thinker. He sees himself leading prayer gatherings in stadiums. He's not too far away from his goal even now as a teenager. As an adult, he will see to it that his life will count for God.

Phil
He has a love for Aboriginal people. He ministers with practical demonstration and a song along with his adopted Aboriginal family.

The stories go on . . . and so do the storytellers.
In reality, these once-little people with big prayers, now big

people with bigger prayers, are, themselves the kaleidoscopes. Full of color and movement. Anticipating the next turn. Never quite sure what it will be like. But one can be certain that their lives will be more beautifully vibrant, more thrilling as the years go by.

Growing Beyond Measure

David (CGPM International Director) says it all:

> In 1991, I was offered a job by Burger King International, to be in charge of their internal design department. One day before I was to go to Homestead, Florida, and confirm the position, Hurricane Andrew made a direct hit and completely destroyed the Burger King office complex there.
>
> Months later when Burger King called me to return there to confirm my position and start working, I felt God say to me, "I do not want you working there; I want you to work with Esther and the Network. What I have planned is *bigger than Burger King!*" A short time later, the Lord started the Children's Global Prayer Movement.

Bigger than Burger King? Absolutely. Interpret it however you see it. *As I see it, anything God does is bigger than anything man does.*

It bears repeating: This movement is very big and getting bigger even as I write and still bigger as you read! As more and more praying WorldShapers emerge (yours among them), their stories, too, will be recorded in history books and in the annals of heaven.

PART THREE

THROUGH THE
EYES OF
God

CHAPTER 8

HERE WE COME,

Ready or Not!

And a little child shall lead them.

ISAIAH 11:6

"Esther, sit down," Mary shouted. "Wait till you hear this!"

Mary had recently returned from the Global Consultation on World Evangelism (GCOWE) planning meeting in Colorado Springs sponsored by the AD2000 and Beyond Movement. She and her husband, Bill, had represented me. She described the following to me: "Dr. Bush and Dr. Wagner burst into the tiny meeting room after a brief break to announce this brilliant God idea. 'We want praying children to be official delegates to the GCOWE, and we want Esther and the CGPM to head up the whole project!'"

I stared into space, took a deep breath and remarked coolly to cover up my apprehension, "Well, God will choose these children. We're sure not going to!"

In two minutes flat, we were on our faces to talk with Him about it. Not that I didn't trust these distinguished men of God; I just wasn't sure of us!

Yet, miraculously, the children began surfacing from all the right places. With reverential awe and a good dose of healthy fear, we began running hard to keep abreast of the momentum (as if we had a choice).

"Satan just hates this, Mary!" I exclaimed more than once during the process, utterly frustrated, mostly in trying to work out logistics. It would take months to bring about this grand-scale assignment. It was something I had absolutely no mind for.

Mary knew exactly what would get me back on track at times like this. "Esther, just think about what it will be like when we'll be praying together with all the children!"

Wise lady.

GOD'S 40 PRAYING CHILDREN

There are certain moments and events that shatter our conventional notions. Such a time happened in 1995 at the Global Consultation on World Evangelism in the Seoul, Korea, convention center.

I had been in a press conference when suddenly a colleague was in my face demanding, "Esther, Esther, you've got to come *right now* to see what's happening with the children!"

Before I could say, "Excuse me," I was abruptly ushered out and down several flights of stairs through a seemingly endless, unadorned passageway to where the children had gathered in a basement garage transformed into a battle station for prayer.

Like a choir's thunderous crescendo, the voices of the 40 praying children of GCOWE '95 echoed repeatedly through the tunnel-like atmosphere. Rushing to the scene, I visualized their command being carried on the wings of the wind, shooting like a dart from the arrow of an expert marksman to its target.

I found the children huddled together, facedown on the floor, crying out in such fervent petition to the Lord that, like a magnet, it had drawn in many adults who either stood reverently by or joined in. Frankly, I had never seen or heard anything quite like it before; but having a strong sense of God's presence enveloping the children, I could only conclude that it was a divinely orchestrated moment and I, with reverential fear of the Lord, had been assigned to guide it.

Approaching the scene, out of breath as I was, the Holy Spirit's anointing on the children hit me like a power surge in a storm. To this day, I quake at the thought of having been plopped right in the middle of those ignited young prayer warriors pounding the gates of heaven and hell!

During the conference while they were praying under a powerful blessing, God had shown two of the children a picture of a virus: ugly, with tentacles. Each drew in detail what it looked like. Their descriptions matched exactly. Later, their image of it was proven clearly accurate when it was compared to a medical book picture of the virus viewed under a microscope. (Remember, I'm just the scribe. But a believing one.)

Three days later, this message from the World Health Organization headlined worldwide media: "Ebola virus in Zaire arrested."

Could it be that the prayers of the children had arrested the virus?

God Shows Up for the Children

The caption read: Children of hope, GCOWE's youngest delegates pray for the world. I smiled as I read the feature article in the GCOWE Today newspaper:

> When the children of the International Children's Prayer Track drop to their knees, God shows up! Wide-eyed and eager, they are ready to take on the world.[1]

This was so true. God showed up for the children. As one child observed,

> In 10 days, we went from the third balcony, back row, on the first day; then to the basement garage for our prayer meetings; but on the last day, we led the processional and ended up on stage, center front! Our praying must have made God really happy!

While I was at the conference, I saw the children prostrate themselves before the Lord. I heard them weep intensely for the lost and engage aggressively in spiritual warfare for up to four hours at times.

I saw the astonishment and ultimate respect from world leaders when children, given the privilege to lay hands on them, prayed and prophesied with astounding wisdom. Visibly moved, many of these distinguished national leaders would say that never before had a child prayed for them. For some, it would be the highlight of the entire event. Imagine!

I saw the resplendent beam on Dr. Wagner's face as the children hovered over him to pray. I heard them shout, "Y-YES!" our seal of agreement after every prayer. I heard Japheth, six, our youngest delegate, declare, "O Lord, this world needs you—a lot!"

(He came to be known as our "a lot" delegate, because he prayed it—a lot!)

No cultural, ethnic, social, age or language barriers interfered with their unity. They were simply happy to be among their ilk—prayer warriors, just doing their job. Our Spanish interpreter was six years old!

Rest and relaxation were not an option. The children's day off would be spent in fasting and prayer. Some would go to the border between North and South Korea to pray. "We came here to pray," they'd say, and that they did—superbly. It confounded and humbled me. I revered them. I cried hard. I'll always remember; I know God will, too. I longed for the whole world to know, to see, to feel.

Dr. Bush and Dr. Wagner had certainly heard accurately from God that day when He placed in them the thought of children intercessors participating in this historic event. The children's presence there among 4,500 world leaders was the most glorious prophetic act one could ever imagine. Their powerful prayers live on. These WorldShapers and I will always be grateful.

"O LORD, THIS WORLD NEEDS YOU—A LOT!"

JAPHETH

God Heard the Children

There we were, about a dozen adults, with those 40 stouthearted soldiers of the Lord. The children's ages ranged from 6 to 15. They came from eight nations (10 others just like them from other nations, with us in spirit). These children proved to be the conference's brightest spot, to the absolute delight and amazement of all. Especially to Dr. Bush, Dr. Wagner and us.

Of course, God wasn't amazed, but I know He was pleased.

The effects in the wake of the GCOWE '95 experience were seen in the hearts of the children. It wasn't long before we began receiving messages from them.

Daniel and Marcus
We're holding prayer meetings with the children at church. We got to pray over the adults, too!

Sara
I'll remember the praying forever. I've started a God's World Club in Indonesia.

Volnei
I'm taking on Brazil! It's my land to conquer.

Ryan
We were commissioned to give children everywhere the anointing to pray. I've spoken in several churches. I got to pray over the children and then they let me pray over the adults! My blessing from Korea gets stronger every day.

Hayden and Phillip
We were invited to spread the message about children and prayer in several churches here in Australia.

Annie
In my school's chapel service I told the children all about Korea and tossed the GLOBALL around. All were eager to pray for the world, some for the first time!

David and Andrew
We want you to pray that doors would open for us to share the vision of prayer with other children in Costa Rica.

Ashlee
I felt the Lord was telling me that the enemy was trying to attack our church. My pastor said that everyone present that night was to be anointed with oil. I anointed all the children. We had a breakthrough. This was my first time to anoint anyone with oil, and it was so *cool!*

Daniel
I went to the Philippines on a summer missions outreach, where God used me after my Korea anointing.

Nicole
I appeared on local TV and shared my GCOWE experience. I've spoken to several youth, children and adult groups already about the vision God gave me about the church in America and how we must pray.

And that's just a small sampling. *Good news. Y-YES!*

God's Timing
In His sovereign genius, God brought together exactly the praying children He had chosen from the foundations of the earth,

announcing to the world, "I am raising up a new generation of young intercessors and prayer warriors for end-time harvest and revival. Make room for them."

Around the year 2025 (if there is one), I can see a communications system—far more sophisticated than the old Internet—with this message flashing on it from one renowned world leader to another on the other side of the planet: "Remember GCOWE '95?"

Note
1. *GCOWE Today,* Saturday, May 20, 1995, p. 5.

CHAPTER 9

WORLDSHAPERS FOR THE

New Millennium

And David [only a boy] said to Goliath, "You come against me with sword

and spear . . . but I come against you in the name of the LORD Almighty!"

1 SAMUEL 17:45

GOD'S POINT OF VIEW

Long before the Worldwide Prayer Movement emerged and before praying children entered my life, I had felt rather lonely in this matter of prayer. For months I lay on my face, alone, in our sanctuary, crying out, "O Lord, where are all the intercessors?"

One unforgettable day, His answer finally came. "Esther, I'm going to turn your heart to the children. That's where you'll find the intercessors I want you to raise up." Having never worked with children in the traditional sense, His words jolted me.

Nevertheless, they trumpeted a sound that stayed locked in my heart until it's time was to come . . . and come, it did!

He assured me that He has birthed in today's children an irrefutable desire to pray. Many of them are world-class intercessors who comprehend global issues and terminology. They utilize the power of Jesus' name with unabashed faith. They don't mince words. They are serious; direct. Their hands are clean; hearts, pure and guileless.

Their prayer warfare in confronting strongholds is bold, audacious, "rightly dividing" the Word. As in, "Now, devil, you hear this! It is written!"

No wonder God has called on them to be end-time prayer warriors.

Pray not Play, Weep not Sleep

Kelly's command had definite overtones of a reprimand. "It's time to pray not play, weep not sleep!" Sounding like a drill sergeant, this 10-year-old veteran intercessor was not at all happy about how things were going. It was three o'clock in the morning. The children were part of an intergenerational prayer gathering that had begun at 8 P.M. and was to run till 8 A.M.

After seven hours of intercession, the children had been going strong in spiritual warfare, praise and celebration. But most of the adults had disappeared when Kelly suddenly grabbed the nearest microphone and blasted this quite alarming wake-up call. Immediately, heads started popping up out of sleeping bags. Bodies began sheepishly reappearing from the break room.

You can be sure Kelly got what she wanted: wide-awake intercessors doing what they came to do—pray! The message was simple: Don't mess with this WorldShaper!

Her message, "It's time to pray not play, weep not sleep" is printed on the backs of our CGPM T-shirts that have gone around the world. Thousands of children have responded to the call. Dads and moms, pastors and children's workers tell us that when their children wear the shirts, it reminds and convicts. One guilt-ridden dad remarked, "I admit it haunts me."

How does it strike you?

A House of Prayer

God cherishes children with zeal to pray. Sometimes that zeal comes in the form of a wake-up call like in Kelly's case, but other times it comes in a creative expression as in the poem below.

> Children cry—see the tears in their eyes?
> The devil has given them such a lie.
> Stop the lie from getting inside.
> Tell the truth! Tell the truth!
>
> Crying children—they need help.
> If only Jesus' love could be felt.
> Tanks and soldiers and fighting out there—
> There's a reason to be a house of prayer!

Four boys, ages 9 and 10, huddled together in the early morning of another 12-hour prayer gathering, penned this poem on a scrap of paper and handed it to me. When Nathan read it aloud, its impact ushered in a wave of intercession that kept us on our faces for a very long time.

The poem became part of our "House of Prayer Rap" which has been sung far and wide. The heart cry of this generation, in part expressed here, will indeed tarry till Jesus comes. Four young lads, WorldShapers who know something of His heart.

God's Wee Intercessor

One of the most memorable moments when I learned age was not an issue with God was with my first child intercessor, Jesse Schnorr. At the time he was only three, a seed God would use for all the others yet to come.

Jesse was born into a home of intercessors, as I was. God had spoken to his parents about his destiny, his purpose. My pastor/husband had dedicated him to the Lord. Jesse was ideally God's chosen one to start me on this journey.

One day this precocious little boy came into my office for his customary treat from my famous candy machine. But this time, his eyes were fixed on a globe. I, of course, was absolutely clueless about this divine setup. I handed him a little soft cloth globe and casually said, "Here Jesse, give all the Jesses in the world a Jesus hug."

He instinctively did as asked. But that wasn't all. Without a premeditated thought, I suggested, "Now, Jesse, why don't you pray for all the three-year-old boys in the world who don't know Jesus." Jesse then did the most amazing thing. He grabbed a bottle of anointing oil from my desk, dabbed a little oil on the globe and hugged it even tighter. A tear trickled down his cheek. He prayed and prayed and prayed, as if everyone in the world were three. By that time I was boo-hooing.

Jesse became one of the 40 GCOWE '95ers. Today, Jesse is a well-seasoned CGPM junior staffer. His father, David, is the CGPM International Director and works superbly with these remarkable children. They returned to South Korea to participate in a nationwide prayer rally for 40,000 children held in the

Seoul Olympic Stadium. Moments like that are important to Jesse because his most fervent prayer is for the reuniting of North and South Korea. He feels that someday he will prayer walk in North Korea.

In God's eyes, that's the prayer of a veteran WorldShaper. Great prayers of faith from the heart of a young boy.

God's Priorities Are Honored

I think God may take note of children's prayers because they so often seem sensitive to His priorities. For instance, many of these remarkable children think it quite incredulous that church people don't know about the 10/40 Window. This reminds me of a great story that happened at our church.

During a church service my husband had invited people with broken lives to receive healing. Some of those who were weeping had wept many times before, never really surrendering. Troubled, I bowed my head and prayed, *Lord, how long will it take? They should be weeping for others by now.*

Then I heard a small stir. As I looked up, the children had unobtrusively moved to a wall-mounted world map. They were totally engrossed in intercession, quietly weeping for the children of the 10/40 Window.

Selah.

God Sees Humility in Children

Tripping over his own feet, Ben, seven, had dashed to the platform, to prophesy and pray.

This is what God says! "Jesus is coming sooner than you think! You'd better be ready!" Oh, God, please, let everyone here be ready.

SHOULD ANY
CHILD BE
DENIED HIS OR
HER INALIENABLE
RIGHT TO BE A
NORMAL PRAYER
WARRIOR TO
SHAPE THE
WORLD GOD'S
WAY?

The congregation, gathered for a Sunday morning worship service, was left totally confounded. Shedding pride, some convicted and willing souls knelt at the altar to repent. Y-YES! A confident and determined young prophet, this WorldShaper!

Yet these children are humble and feel honored to be in God's prayer army. Best of all, they're happy, well balanced, free, because they're freed to cast the cares of the world on Him. So, then, should any child be denied his or her inalienable right to be a normal prayer warrior to shape the world God's way?

Judging by the accounts I receive from around the world, the children I profile are typical of millions just like them—your children possibly among them. A growing army of young prayer warriors dead set on making a difference. I've interacted personally with many of them.

GOD'S CONCLUSIONS

So what must God see when He hears young children exhibiting such great faith? Here's what I think.

A Brilliant Leader Among WorldShapers

In 1996 Nicole, 12, profoundly stated her spiritual experiences while in Washington, DC, for the National Day of Prayer and in similar events that followed:

Some might remember; I'll never forget. Remember when we prayed against abortion? When we broke the spirit of racism off the people? How about when we were sitting in the circle weeping over the nation we loved, that had fallen so far? These and many more are memories that will relive themselves day after day in our minds, of the week of Washington for Jesus.

Recognized as children of power, equipped and ready to use what was ours through the blood of Jesus, we waged war for the freedom of our nation . . . a nation that had lived and accepted the bondage of Pharoah. Pornography. Homosexuality. Abortion. Racism. AIDS, Occultism. HIV. We stomped over all these and more, placing the enemy under our feet as we did spiritual warfare over the map of our country. We shouted, we declared, we proclaimed that each and every state would turn back to God.

Our prayer times consisted of heartfelt pleas to our Father to heal our land, awaken the hearts of the lost and revive the souls of the righteous. We demanded the devil to release his hold on the nation. "You have no right, devil...you've already lost...those unborn children don't belong to you! They are Christ's."

There were major breakthroughs in our lives as a group as well. In May 1995 at GCOWE, in Seoul, Korea, we started out praying at the bottom of the Torch Conference Center in the parking garage, but by the end of the conference God had moved us to the front row of the general assembly.

By April of 1996 at Washington for Jesus, our group of praying children was recognized from the first day. We were received as mighty prayer warriors in God's hand for winning our nation back over to Christ. God is awesome! Praise Him for what He did through us to change the course of this nation's history.

A Passionate WorldShaper

Blake, 10, made it very clear that he couldn't wait. "Oh, Mom, I've got to pray for souls! Right now!" The mother described what happened:

> The evening church service had run very late and we were in the car going home. A spirit of intercession suddenly came upon him. So I turned right around and took him straight to the home of our church's head intercessor. We prayed with him until he felt a release several hours later.

A WorldShaper in the Making

> Oh, Lord, I know I have to stop, but I just can't stop praying! I just can't stop! O, help me, Jesus!

Ever hear a plea like this? (I didn't think so.) It came from Jonathan, seven, an orphan in Uganda whose parents had died of AIDS. A CGPM team had gone to the orphanage to train the children—all 800 of them—to pray for orphans just like themselves all over the world. His own prayer had overwhelmed him. It had never happened before.

Selah

I think the Lord wants us to pause and reflect upon what He is doing among the children today. It is clear to me that God wants to use godly children as WorldShapers.

To parents, pastors, educators and Sunday School workers, sensitive to His hand working through the children, I say just let the children pray. Think about these things.

Selah.

Think about God's call to prayer for every child.

Selah.

God is calling for WorldShapers.

FOR SUCH A TIME
as This

Thanks to my text tweakers, Sarah and Mary, and the Regal Books experts, all for now at least, has been said. However, here's my last word.

Speaking the Truth

You have no idea how many times while trekking through the bailiwick of children and prayer, that I've cried out in trepidation, "Oh, God, what have I done?"

His answer? "How many times do I have to tell you, Esther; putting it that way, you have done nothing, except to say yes to me. Don't take credit; leave the rest with Me."

Nonetheless, I've vacillated between "lion" and "chicken" while writing this book. (Should I say it like this or like that?

Should I soften it to make it more palatable, more widely acceptable? Have I gone too far? Not far enough? Is it strong enough? Too strong? Did I do justice to praying children? Will I be seen as a viable teacher of praying children? Will people really find all this believable?)

In my ambivalence, the Lord seemed always to say, "Esther, just tell the truth."

Each time I've sat at my computer, before clicking on the Shortcut to Book icon, I've prayed a prayer paraphrased from verse 6 of Malachi 2: *Lord, please let the law of truth be found in me. Let equity come from my lips.*

Then there's that first line of my parents' poem to their "Beloved Esther": "Your calling is the best."

So how could I keep it to myself? The truth I had hidden in my heart and stashed away in boxes and files about children and prayer—that "best calling"—is now out, for such a time as this. Y-YES!

Urgency and Wisdom

Let the little people go! The appeal comes from my heart, but I hear God saying it to all of us—as in the biblical account of Moses petitioning the Pharaoh on behalf of the Israelites held in bondage in Egypt.

So, to me, unleashing this generation of praying children and their powerful prayers comes just in time—and is doable— for such a time as this. Y-YES!

SUGGESTED
Reading

- Beason, Helen. *Children of Purpose*. City and state unknown: Living Word Church, 1995.
- Christiansen, Evelyn. *What Happens When Children Pray*. Colorado Springs: Chariot Victor Publishing, 1997.
- Chun, Clarine. *Not Without the Children*. Kedah, West Malaysia: Superkids Ministry, 1995.
- Fuller, Cheri. *When Mothers Pray*. Sisters, OR: Multnomah Publishers, Inc., 1997.
- Klibourn, Phyllis, ed. *Children in Crisis*. City and state unknown: MARC Publications, 1996.
- Graham, Franklin. *Kids Praying for Kids*. Nashville, TN: Tommy Nelson Publishers, 1998.
- Layton, Barry and Dian. *Soldiers with Little Feet*. Shippensburg, PA: Destiny Image, 1989.

- Morgan, Dr. Patricia. *How to Raise Children of Destiny.* Shippensburg, PA: Destiny Image Publishers, 1994.
- Walters, David. *Equipping the Younger Saints.* Macon, GA: Good News Fellowship Ministries, 1993.
- ———. *Kids in Combat.* Macon, GA: Good News Fellowship Ministries, 1989.

RESOURCES FOR

Children

PRAYERTOOLS© are fun to pray with (in the spirit of joy referred to in Isaiah 56:7)! Each tool is designed to help parents, teachers and pastors encourage and nurture the value of prayer in their children. All materials come in English (some are also available in Spanish).

Instructional Book

What About the Children? by Esther Ilnisky

This is an instruction book that covers all the basics in cultivating a prayerful heart in children. Ilnisky offers insights into how children need to pray to their Father. This is a perfect resource for any pastor, leader or parent who wants to nurture children in understanding God's presence.

GLOBALL

This delightful soft ball has "Catch the Vision" written on it. You'll be smiling and laughing with the children. Each child tosses this soccerball-sized tool to another saying "Catch the vision—get global!" Order the ball alone or purchase the GLOB-ALL kit that provides easy-to-read instructions on how to make your own GLOBALL. Excellent tool for any child—from toddlers to high schoolers. Even adults get into the action.

WorldShaper Squeeze Ball

Small, soft, rubber ball with the "Catch the Vision" theme printed on it. This tool is squeezed to make an "impression" by prayer. It is great for small groups or individual children to use as they pray. Wonderful resource for grades 1 through 12.

Prayer Spinner Game

This simple game allows children's spinner to focus on issues important to any country (the national version) and around the world (the global version, i.e., unreached people). Perfect for toddlers, kindergarten and grades 1 through 4; but it fascinates everyone.

"House of Prayer" CD, Cassette, Sheet Music

This musical bonanza has exciting tunes including such favorites as "House of Prayer March" (a rap version as well), "Window of the World" and "Catch the Vision." Children come alive while singing and learn about prayer through words and motions. Great for toddlers, kindergarten and grades 1 through 4.

Videos

CGPM offers three wonderful videos that cover basic instructional material for helping children become committed prayer warriors; events at GCOWE '95 in Seoul, Korea; and the amazing Washington for Jesus '96 rally with children fervently praying for the welfare of the nation.

Banners

We offer two banners made out of vinyl-covered tarp material that is durable and weatherproof. Graphics are in full color. One banner displays "I am a House of Prayer for all the Nations!" with a colorful, cheerful house graphic; the other banner displays "Catch the Vision! Get Global!" with various outstretched children's hands running along the bottom length of the banner. Both banners come in two sizes: 10' x 32' and 7' x 32'.

Additional Materials

CGPM offers numerous other tools (T-Shirts, hats, manuals, books, etc.). To inquire about these materials, to order items or for further information, contact:

Esther Network International
854 Conniston Road
West Palm Beach, Florida 33405-2131
U.S.A.
Phone: 561-832-6490
Fax: 561-832-8043
Web Address: www.cgpm.org
E-mail: cgpmeni@mindspring.com

Best-Sellers from Regal

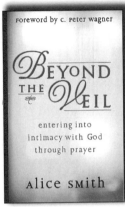
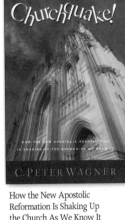
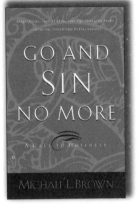
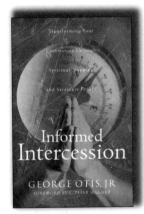
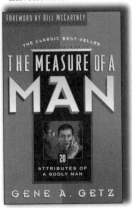
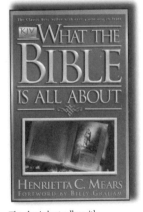

Best-Sellers
from Regal

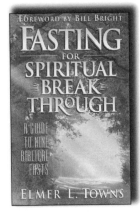
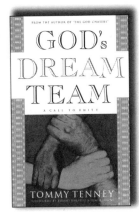
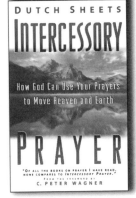

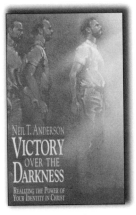
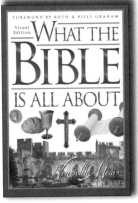